ONE HUG
AT A TIME

ONE HUG AT A TIME

99 STORIES FROM THE MAN
WHO EMBRACED THE WORLD

DAVID HALE SYLVESTER

To my mother, Thank you for telling me that I was strong enough, smart enough, and willful enough to figure my way out of any situation. I have; and everyone should be so fortunate to have someone as marvelous as you in their life.

To anyone I've ever hugged, your embrace was a portal to my becoming a better man.

Contents

Foreword

So, you've decided to read David Sylvester's book, *One Hug at a Time*. Lucky you! Or maybe it's more than luck. Perhaps a friend recommended this book or a friend of a friend. Or, even better, a random stranger thought you needed some no-nonsense happiness. Or maybe you read a news article or a blog or listened to stories about this dude who travels around the world just to hug and high-five folks. Or maybe you heard him speak about the death of his friend in the World Trade Center and how David honored his life by riding across the U.S. It's possible you stumbled across *davidhalesylvester. com*, read about his Australian *Hugs and High-Fives Tour*, and were wowed to discover he biked, hugged, high-fived, and volunteered his way from Sydney to Melbourne all while being tormented by kangaroos, spiders, flies, wildfires, and wicked sciatic pain. Perchance you read his first book, *Traveling at the Speed of Life*, and followed his path across the U.S., Africa, and Asia, inspired by his honesty, humor, and dauntless spirit. Or maybe you needed a book to make sense (and fun) of a seemingly senseless world. It's also quite likely you are among the fortunate many who have met David, have high-fived or been hugged by him, felt the air squeezed from your lungs as he swept you into his Herculean arms, and your life has not been quite the same since.

If you haven't met David, you'll get to know him on these pages. He's full of surprises; a man who takes risks, loves food, dogs, people, and is unstoppable in his quest to motivate humanity—ALL of humanity. I've known him for 20 years, and while reading this book, I often felt like I was meeting him for the first time. He's a brash man from Philadelphia who curses—a lot. He's a body-builder, trainer, writer, bike rider, world traveler, motivational speaker, and he wasn't always a 'hugger.' In an early chapter, "Eulogy," you'll meet a younger David wriggling out of his father's embrace. At the time he was a high school senior, "too old for such displays of affection." And you'll meet his father, envy David for having such a dad, and get a glimpse of what makes David want to hug and high-five the world. You'll see David finding wisdom in being chased by a 'night soil' truck, taunted by children, stalked by a wild dog, and arrested (mistakenly). You'll also understand why it is, (to riff off Caveman who you'll meet in the book), that even though David, "curses all the time and made up this goofy huggin' shit, all types of people—parents, teachers, students, men who don't hug men, soldiers, exotic dancers, AND kids—love him and WANT his black ass to keep talking." And I'll also add, "Keep hugging and keep writing." Please.

In this book, you'll find David's world. It is brave, heartfelt, funny, astonishing, delightful, irreverent, generous, and disarmingly kind. I offer one piece of advice—truthfully it's David's advice: While reading this book, keep in mind this is YOUR world, too. So heat up the teapot or fill a glass with ice and something nice; snap open a bag of chips or slice up an apple that's crisp. Tell your friends, 'Tomorrow,' your kids to 'Chill out,' and your dog to 'Lie down.' Close the door, turn off your phone, find the most comfortable chair, bed, bench, or couch. Stretch out or curl up and get ready to be hugged by David's stories and the people in YOUR world. You'll never be quite the same again.

Sheryl Leonard
Writer, teacher, hugger

Introduction

I was fortunate enough to be the recipient of a "David Sylvester Signature Hug" back in 2004 when he was visiting mutual friends in California. As a life-long hugger myself, I knew this hug was more nourishing than most. Not just because of David's stature compared to my smaller frame, what struck me was the hug contained a beautiful dose of love and caring energy that has always stuck with me to this day.

For almost two decades since that wholesome hug, I followed David's amazing bike and hug and high5 journeys through Africa, Asia, Israel and the U.S. It was incredible to watch him share kindness and goodwill with almost every human he encountered—even some who were not so sure of this big, out-spoken dude from Philly from the US of A! But his infectious smile and desire to engage EVERYONE was certain to be a success even if it wasn't reported on the national news—this guy was DOING something about true human connection!

While most of us were isolating and becoming addicted to our mobile devices, David was actively dispelling the belief that "people are evil" by engaging their better angels even while his heart was still aching over losing two men who meant the world to him. By proving the world was not the bad, scary place we were told, David freed others to laugh, smile, hug and connect. His life's work came out of a collective pain and we are all better for it.

Fast forward to 2021, and I was given the wonderful opportunity to co-edit and collaborate with David on *One Hug at a Time*. I am amazed by his commitment to embody true grace and kindness and have been fortunate enough to read his favorite selection of stories from his epic journeys. They made me laugh, cry and cheer. This book is truly the human experience in written form to be enjoyed for what it is: a beautiful collection of multi-cultural human connections encompassing all walks of life.

I believe this book is best consumed with an open mind and open heart. Dip in to read a chapter or two or binge the entire book for a healthy dose of good Rx. NOTE: Get ready to laugh as David is not afraid of humor and ridicule! You may also shed a few tears as some stories get you in the feels, but that's the POINT!

Best wishes on your reading adventure with Ambassador, David Sylvester as your guide,

—Mary Sandor

A Simple Hug

Hi, my name David Hale Sylvester and I would like to thank you for picking up this book.

To explain why I believe this One Hug at a Time is necessary now, let me first tell you what a hug feels like to me.

You know the feeling when you find some money in the pocket of a pair of jeans?

No matter the denomination, 1–$100, the found bills leave you feeling like you discovered treasure.

That's precisely how I feel when getting a hug or a high5 from a passerby.

Since 2001, I have traveled through 50 states and 42 countries, amassing over half a million pieces of this treasure.

I didn't realize that hugs would become my life currency at the beginning of that year, but on September 11, embraces became priceless to me.

On that day, I believe that hugs became more precious to everyone.

Without cell phones and social media permeating every aspect of our lives, we didn't look down on a device to provide comfort and community.

We instead turned to each other to find some reassurance that our future wasn't as dire as the crumbling Twin Towers made it look.

In 2002 I honored my friend Kevin Bowser's life by biking from Washington State to Philadelphia, hugging everyone, and something happened.

The soothing embrace of the nation left me thinking that hugs might become my new life currency. But that sounded foolish, to even me.

I needed to do more research and did so by bicycling from Cairo to Cape Town.

The received hugs, smiles, and humanity turned my Africa trip into a once-in-a-lifetime experience spurred on visions of acquiring even more treasure.

I bicycled Asia next, and though pedaling from Istanbul to Beijing was much more of a challenge than any other trip, I returned home wanting more treasure and knowing that I was willing to work for it.

My work for more treasure began when ESPN contacted me to write a piece about my travels.

Writing for ESPN was a massive opportunity, but I knew that I had to find another way to connect with their readership without being a professional athlete, rich, young, famous, or sponsored like other people featured on their network. So, in going with Freud's "out of your vulnerabilities will come your strength," I wrote with brutal honesty about my search for hugs, high5s, and smiles.

People loved my honesty and "hugged" me through their correspondence.

Emails from around the world filled my inbox with people sharing how they were inspired. One note I received months after the article published was indeed a treasure.

It was a note and bracelet from a woman who said her mother had had cancer and read my article every time she went to chemotherapy. Each reading ushered in a smile, and the woman thanked me for living a life that brought her mother happiness during a painful time when nothing else did. She also informed me that her mother had passed away and felt that she would want me to have one of her bracelets. She ended the note: "Keep Going."

Putting the bracelet on my wrist made me cry.

I wasn't alone in this treasure hunt.

Hugs, high5s, and good vibes was the life currency for others too.

To celebrate this, I bicycled from San Diego to Philadelphia and added the element of stopping each week to volunteer a day at a local shelter and charitable organization.

It was beautiful.

Each week, I had a dialogue with a very different population who observed something different in me and, in turn, asked for something different from me.

I returned home from that tour with a stronger sense of self and purpose and feeling like I put on a pair of old jeans and discovered a treasure in every pocket!

Pockets full of treasure make one feel fearless, so even though I had only written articles before, I wrote the book *Traveling at the Speed of Life*.

I bicycled the U.S. again to celebrate its publication, but I treated this tour differently by speaking less and listening more, and all I heard was, "You know you aren't done, right?"

Being Hug-Wealthy but cash-poor made this notion seem absurd, but the people were correct, and I soon found myself bicycling Australia for my first official Hug and High 5 Tour.

Successfully bicycling from Sydney to Melbourne, volunteering at a few charities, and embracing 1,000 people in a month was a big step for me. I attempted to replicate this experience by pedaling across the U.S. in 2016. But a sinus and ear infection stopped me from cycling.

But at this point in my story, nothing could stop my treasure hunting, though!

That summer, I drove across the country, deliberately seeking out people to hug who didn't look like me, think like me, or vote like me. And I was aggressive at it, embracing a real scary dude with a few tattoos in that Nazi font and embracing other people wearing confederate flag clothing.

I was determined to create good moments in the country and felt accomplished by the tour's end. But The Pulse nightclub massacre occurred a day later, letting me know that there was still much more to do.

I traveled to Orlando, embracing everyone I could. The generated warmth carried me through to offer hugs at the Republican National Convention in Cleveland, the Democratic National Convention in Philadelphia, and other places.

By 2016's end, I had embraced people in 31 states and wanted to forge ahead.

So, in 2017, I decided to be proactive and create good news for people by staging Hug-Parties.

The first party was on Valentine's Day at the country's geographic heart in Lebanon, Kansas, and was terrific because I hugged 105 of the town's 195 residents. But what profoundly touched me was that a Wyoming man drove 400 miles to get a hug. Wearing an expression of disbelief mixed with honor, I stood motionless as the man hugged me and said, "I believe in what you are doing. Keep going."

This moment was so impactful that I partnered with Duke Cannon Soap in the summer of 2017 for the Big Dave Hugs America Tour. I hugged, high5'd, and positively connected with 13,986 people in 48 states in 77 days on that tour. The trip was a bounty of treasure that left me ever hopeful, and I continued to build upon that energy by offering hugs of support after the shootings in Las Vegas, Sutherland Springs, and Nashville.

Some people thought this would all be a passing fancy, but I've continued staging hug parties throughout North America, Europe, and Israel with the hope of doing more.

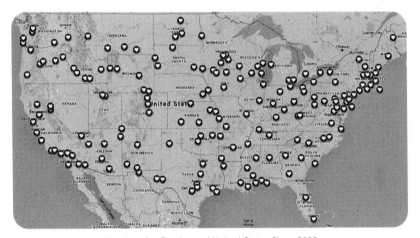

Hugging the Continental United States Since 2002

Then 2020 happened.

COVID. Uncertainty. Forced unemployment. Fear mongering. Quarantines. Social distancing. Murder. Protests. Riots. Intense political discord. Lions—Tigers—Bears—Oh my!!

Seemingly overnight, the entire world was thrust into a world devoid of hope and brightness.

Some things like Zoom Calls allowed us to see each other and be somewhat productive, giving us glimmers of light, but it wasn't enough.

Each day, there was another birth, death, wedding, and major life events that isn't complete until there's a hug of congratulations, comfort, consolation, or community that passed by without any contact.

Every day of 2020 solidified the realization that our COVID-year of 2020 was much worse than 9/11 because it snatched from us the very thing needed to ease our pain and anxiety: human connection.

We also learned that no app, hashtag, or virtual reality platform could ever replace a hug regardless of how clever.

Soon, people from around the planet began messaging me, wondering what the current societal climate would do to my "hug business."

It was incredibly touching for people to be concerned about my hugs and efforts to share them in the world. But with social distancing, I was sidelined from doing what I did best when the world needed it most . . or was I?

One of my old bosses used to yell, "there's no excuse for doing nuthin'!" at me all the time, and that mantra took hold in my psyche because, isolated on my porch, I scoured my memory and began furiously scribbling short hug stories from my travels.

I wrote stories I believed would make any reader laugh, cry, and feel the hope and warmth of humanity missing from our lives.

I wrote stories I believed would make anyone smile.

Writing about these moments inspired me to come up with another trip, the #SmileWithBigDave Tour.

On this tour, I drove the continental 48 states doing good deeds for people in each state—masked and socially distant—to create one more smile in the world.

Many called me foolish for doing this tour, and I was admittedly fearful of COVID but living in a world where hugs and human contact were scarce yet crucial scared me even more.

The emotions I encountered were real and raw, from speaking to a North

Carolina man who couldn't attend his brother's funeral to meeting an Oregon woman with cancer who doubted if she would ever get to hold her newborn grandchild overseas and more.

By the time I completed my 12,000 mile trip on January 5, 2021, I felt good about helping people smile more but needed rest.

I looked forward to quarantining because it would allow me the time to write and share uplifting stories. Instead, I sat riveted to the television, looking at the horrific events at the Capitol.

To live a life that has allowed me to travel throughout 50 U.S. states and 42 countries to seek out and embrace half a million people ranging from newborns to people as old as 101 years old has been an honor indeed.

Each encounter has allowed me the privilege to focus on the promise and potential of who we can be.

But the memories of the America I have experienced violently clashed with grotesque ugliness playing out at the country's heart, and my attempt to reconcile the two brought me to tears.

It also made me rethink the treasure metaphor that I have often used.

Treasure is much too trite and ephemeral of a description.

Traditional treasure hunts for money or fame generally corrupt and appeals to one's worst qualities.

But, to acquire just one more embracing piece of "hug treasure," I have had to evolve in every way possible to become more professional, more productive, more approachable, even more, open and honest.

In many ways, acquiring a simple hug has been my portal for becoming a better man.

Hugs are more than a simple treasure.

Hugs are an essential part of a happy life and the best part of who we can be.

While it was painful to watch T.V. on January 6, 2021, it didn't dissuade me at all.

Seeing insurrection strengthened my resolve and convinced me not to stop hugging people until you see the world as I see it, full of smiles, promise, and potential.

So read some of the 99 short stories on these pages and join me in embracing others.

Start with your family, expand your hug circle to your friends, and then offer a hug to someone you don't know.

Do this so we can all walk away with a shared smile and joint mission of making the world better One Hug at a Time.

Enjoy!!

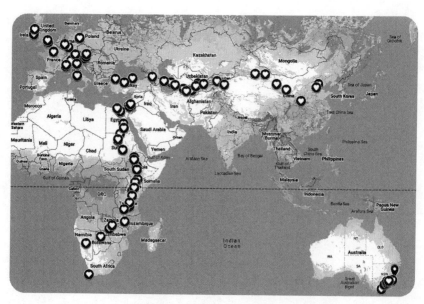

Hugging the World Since 2004

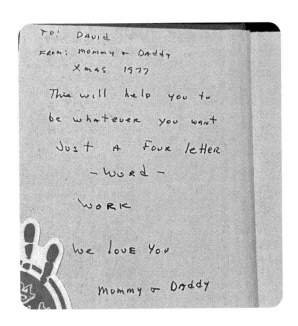

To: DAVID
FROM: mommy + Daddy
Xmas 1977

This will help you to
be whatever you want
Just a four letter
- word -

WORK

We love you

Mommy + Daddy

4-Letter Words Work

Philadelphia, Pennsylvania. Christmas.

I have been cursing for a long time—maybe since 4th grade.

One day at the beginning of the school year, I was on the phone cursing up a storm to a friend, and my dad walked in, and I just KNEW that he caught me.

But my father didn't say a word and just walked through the room, giving me that dreaded "parental stare." You know that look, the "you know you done fucked up" look.

But my father never said anything, so I thought I got away with cursing and never thought about it again UNTIL Christmas.

In addition to Christmas toys, I always got an educational gift of some sort, and this dictionary was one of the gifts.

I always groaned when seeing these gifts, but I knew something was up when my dad said, "Open it up!"

I opened it up to see his handwriting:

> *This will help you to be whatever you want*
> *—just a four-letter word:*
>
> *W-O-R-K*
>
> *We Love You*
>
> *Mommy and Daddy*

I looked up to see my father staring right at me and knew that he had been sitting on this gift and message since September when he heard me curse.

He didn't say anything and just blew out a puff of smoke and nodded his head.

I don't have any of the toys that I got that year—or any year for that matter.

But I still have and refer to this dictionary all the time.

I don't look up words in this book anymore; I just open it up to see my father's handwriting again, read the message and then get the fuck to W-O-R-K!

I miss you, Daddy.

A Coach's Vision

Temple University.

I was a walk-on with the Temple University Football Team, and Super Bowl 55 winning coach Bruce Arians of the Tampa Bay Buccaneers was my coach.

Todd Bowles, Todd McNair, and Keith Armstrong were my Temple teammates and are now on the Super Bowl-winning Tampa Bay coaching staff.

One day my dad came to watch Temple's practice, and afterward, he said that he was going to talk to BA—that's what we called Coach Arians.

Right before walking over, I asked my father to find out if I had a chance to get some playing time.

My dad walked over to BA, and they began talking and laughing like they were old buds or something—it was crazy.

I watched all of this, and then I saw BA put his hand on my dad's shoulder and say something that made my dad wipe his eyes.

"Is he crying??" I thought.

Moments later, my dad walks over to me, wiping away a tear.

"What happened??" I belted out.

Still wiping his eyes, he sniffed and said, "He said that you were okay as a ballplayer but an All-American as a man."

Young and obtuse to the weight of BA's words, I said, "Yeah, but when am I gonna get some clock?"

My father gave me the "dude; you TOTALLY missed the point of what just happened" look and said, "you may be an All-American, but you sure can be dumb too."

He then smiled, gave me a hug and kiss, and told me that he would see me later.

From that day on—up until his death—if he ever saw BA's name in the paper—my father would look at me and point to Coach's name in the newspaper and proudly declare, "That man saw greatness in you."

After my dad died, I continued smiling whenever I saw BA's name because he made my dad smile.

During Tampa Bay's playoff run of 2020, I smiled a lot, and as I saw BA hoist the Lombardi trophy over his head, I smiled, thinking of my father, and had a good cry.

BA, thank you for observing any "All-American" qualities I exhibited as a young man and being kind enough to share them with my father.

You gave my dad a smile.

You gave me a moment I will never forget.

Congrats on the win.

T for Temple U!!!

Why Is the Next Chapter So Long??

Most of *One Hug at a Time*'s stories are short—under 1000 words. But the next chapter, "Eulogy," comes in at a whopping 4000 words and is taken directly from my first book, *Traveling at the Speed of Life*.

Including that chapter wasn't in my original plan, but I remembered a promise I made to a young man shortly after *Traveling at the Speed of Life* came out.

While lecturing Dr. Aimee Glocke's Black Literature class at Cal State, Northridge, one male student expressed his love for my book and said that it was the first book he ever re-read. "You tell good stories," he said.

Flattered to get such a compliment, I began to ask what his favorite chapter was and he excitedly said, "The one about your dad; I loved that one! Your father was a great man."

"I thought so," I said.

In fielding more of the class' questions, the topic of me writing another book came up. Still, on a high from completing my first book, I smiled and said, "One day…maybe…I certainly have more stories."

The first student perked up and said, "Well, if you write another book, you have to put that chapter about your dad in that book too."

I responded by saying something to the effect of "new book—new insights" and when I did, the student snapped, "NO, you can't do that!"

Shocked by the student's edginess, I said, "We'll see."

The next day, I gave another lecture that was open to the whole university this time. The same student from the day before was in attendance, asking the same questions about the chapter about my father and I gave him the same answers. After the lecture was over, I noticed that the student was waiting around so I approached him.

He immediately apologized for being curt with me the day before and said, "Look, I never met my dad. I never knew a dad could mean that much. I never knew that you could love a man that much. I never knew this shit really existed. I would re-read the chapter about your dad and cry, but then I stopped crying, and now I smile because I know that there are good men like him out there. THIS IS WHY you need to put that chapter in your book—new readers may miss out on the magic of your dad. Promise me."

Not expecting so much emotion from this encounter, I casually tried to sidestep it all by saying, "Dude, I don't know." The words barely escaped my mouth when I noticed that the student began to cry. While wiping away tears, he again said, "Promise me—your dad is really that important."

With that, I gave him my word and a really big hug.

Before walking away, he thanked me again for being me and said that my book "really got to him" and inspired him to write poetry for the first time. With that, he handed me a piece of paper that was folded in two and said, "I guess that we wrote this." We hugged again, and as he left, I opened up the paper and saw a poem entitled "Things I Should Not Write About"—about his hardships as a child and his moving beyond them.

Meeting this young man "really got to me," so the next chapter is long, but necessary for me to keep my word.

For the new readers, I hope that you enjoy it. For those re-reading it, I hope you enjoy it even more this time.

Eulogy

Any story about my life that attempts to explain who I am must include the day I journeyed from pew to podium to eulogize my father. I was 27 then and on that day, openly acknowledged to friends, family and perfect strangers that I felt adrift and was going to need my father—all of them.

You see, while your average person may get one father, I had three.

First, I knew Daddy.

Daddy always had three things with him: a lot of charisma, a perspective—giving life lessons for every person he encountered, and a cigarette.

All of that combined and gave him something that all great men have: presence. His fantastic presence was larger than life and made me want to study him in every way; from how he spoke down to his signature fist pump and the words he used to end every conversation with: 'Be good.'

Daddy could do anything.

A great basketball player in his day, Daddy was more excited than I was when I made my 7th-grade basketball team. His face lit up immediately and soon, he was putting on a dribbling display around the house, using the living room furniture as defenders.

In that moment, there was an energy and exuberance about my father that I had never experienced that the walls of the house couldn't contain. He must have felt it too because he said, "Let's go outside."

Once outside, he performed a few more tricks including a tap-drill where you shoot the ball onto a spot about ten feet high and then jump up and tip it back to the same place with the same hand. He did all of this with a lit cigarette dangling from his lip.

As an adult, I can look back on this and remember the huffing and puffing as he talked about how his jump shot could "never" be taken away from him. But when I was a kid, his display left me amazed and a bit overwhelmed—wondering if any of Daddy's spark, athleticism, and magic was in me too.

It wasn't—at least not at that point.

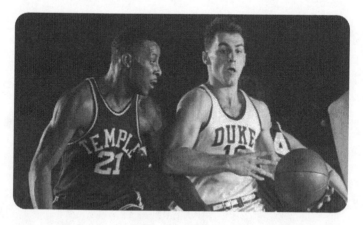

After a few weeks of riding the bench, I finally got in a game and was excited, maybe too excited. My heart pounded furiously as every word of sports advice I had ever heard screamed in my head. Initially, my mouth was dry and my legs felt heavy, but as the game went on, I began to feel more in control and that's when I saw my opportunity.

My opponent mistook my anxiety for lack of skill and got sloppy with his ball handling. I stole the ball from him, ran down the court, and beautifully laid it up for two points.

I then pumped my fist—just like Daddy—and felt like I was on top of the world.

I turned to look at him in the stands, only to find an almost expressionless stare on his face. I then wheeled around to look at my bench of team-mates and coaches, each of whom sat with the same glassy-eyed gaze. Even the referee stood silent for a moment. Everyone looked this way because, in my eagerness to make the play and be "Daddy-like," I didn't dribble the ball AT ALL, except for the one bounce that I did before I laid the ball up.

And if that wasn't bad enough, I argued the call.

Daddy and the rest of my family were natural competitors at everything, from debates to cards. He would tell me that once you got in an opponent's head, the competition was over. So, to ignite the same competitive fire in me, he was merciless while beating me in any game we played.

"All day," was just one of the things that he would say with a wry smile and a glint in his eye while non-stop trash-talking with me as we competed. Then, just as he beat me, he'd stop to say, "Think, David. Remember everything and do differently next time." Then he would repeat the same move in the same way, over and over, until I learned to defend it. Even while watching sports, he would remind me that all great competitors remained focused, at all times, on what was going on in the game.

But, at that time, I was an underachieving schoolboy so the concept of paying attention to anything all the time—let alone paying attention to everything all of the time—seemed a Herculean task.

I never really got what he was saying until much later in life.

How a person thought and what they thought about was a big deal to my entire family. Each day, as a part of my parents' homework—not my regular schoolwork—I had to read a newspaper and be prepared to weigh in on any local, national, or social issues with my family at dinner. Being the youngest didn't afford me any breaks. Neither did my position at the kitchen table.

My marvelous, caring, and intelligent mother sat to my right. My sister, who embodied intellectual excellence, sat across from me. My father sat to my left.

Each conversation slowly, still much too fast for me, made its way around the dinner table, making me feel like I was in the crosshairs. I had to say something because if I didn't have an opinion, defending my apathy was a harder argument. So, I developed an ability to grasp an issue's broadest concepts and would choose a position.

As a kid, I was obsessed with action heroes, but Daddy appreciated men who thought while taking action and always pointed out the vast differences between them. Whether talking about an athlete, activist, or artist, my father would say, "Talent isn't enough in this world," and then give glowing words only to those who leveraged their talent to do something more. "You can't just take. You have to give something back." he'd say.

Daddy was both a thoughtful and thought-provoking man.

He was Daddy to me, but to everyone else, he was Mr. Sam.

Mr. Sam was an esteemed professor at the University of Pennsylvania, School of Social Work. Though I saw him every day, I never truly appreciated him until seeing him through the lens of others. From the university President to the custodial workers and on down to the students, Mr. Sam strolled the campus, acknowledging everyone and was always ready to share a bit of wisdom and a smile.

When I was 17, I was in two different summer basketball leagues and barely knew when one of my teams was practicing for a game, and the other was playing a game. After committing a dumb foul during one game, I heard a familiar voice yell, "Think. Think. Think," amidst the grandstands. As I watched my opponent take his second foul shot, I had convinced myself that my father's voice was permanently resonating throughout my subconscious.

But then, I happened to glance up in the bleachers and see my father, standing there holding a rolled-up newspaper and talking to the gym custodian. "Think," he shouted again with a cigarette dangling from his mouth. Stunned to see him, I stood motionless as play resumed and asked my father how he knew when and where I was playing.

"I've told you your whole life," he yelled across the court. "You don't know WHO I know. Now get your head in the game."

When I spoke to the custodian later about my father, he just laughed and said, "I've known Mr. Sam for a long time."

Mr Sam also cared about my friends and was relentless at engaging them in debates as well. They loved him because he gave a damn. Where I saw Daddy, my friends saw Mr. Sam, a man who cared a lot. And, while many fathers would only cheer and encourage their sons, Mr. Sam yelled for all of us to play our best and always to keep thinking.

After a football game in my senior year of high school, Daddy hugged and kissed me. Believing myself too old for such displays of affection, and flush with teenage bravado, I pushed him away. Suddenly, my friend Ray Sisco hit me in the head with his football helmet and said, "Don't do that to Mr. Sam!" I told Ray that he didn't understand because my dad hugs me all the time.

Ray retorted, "Nah, Beef [my nickname at the time]. YOU don't understand. Some of us have no one coming to our games."

Everyone found Mr. Sam funny, but when he thought that we were bordering on being disrespectful, he was quick to remind us that he was no joke. He would say that his roots were on the rough and tough corners of South Philly and that he could "go back there in a second," if we kept acting up.

When I was 18, I walked into the house to see a friend speaking with my father.

I had no idea what they were talking about but could tell from their body language that the topic was intense. My dad told me to go up to my room, and the two of them ended up speaking for hours until I fell asleep.

Neither of them ever told me what they spoke of that night, but many years later, my friend opened up about being sexually abused and needing to talk with someone. At an age when most young men wouldn't speak to anyone, especially another male, this boy sought out and talked to Mr. Sam. I still run into this friend from time to time and, before we part, he always hugs me and says, "Thank God for Mr. Sam."

Even those who never met him appreciated and admired him. A college classmate raised by a single mother only knew my father through my countless stories. One day she took me aside and said I naturally smiled whenever I spoke of my father which highlighted the story and made her feel like she really had missed out on something essential in her life.

Even when not physically present, Mr. Sam had a way of leaving an indelible mark on lives.

In being a good "Daddy" to me, Mr. Sam became a father and friend to many.

Everyone got an opportunity to enjoy Daddy and benefit from Mr. Sam, but I alone met Samuel.

I met Samuel Sylvester after his cancer diagnosis.

Samuel showed me life from the vantage point of someone who wasn't going to be alive much longer, so there was no holding back.

Our conversations were like no other we had before. Now they were a spontaneous mix of hugs, tears, memories, and his sharing of life lessons. Though many of the life-lessons he communicated were hard to grasp at the time, they were impossible for me to forget because we both knew that these were going to be our last moments together.

Samuel was beautifully human during this time, and another layer of our relationship quickly developed, something much more profound than father and son or even friends. He solidified his presence as my enduring hero because he displayed the best and most essential qualities that a man can show.

Bravery—Because even though he was scared, he demonstrated bravery as he moved forward through his disease.

Honesty and Intelligence—Because when it mattered most, he admitted what he didn't know about life.

Generosity—Because he freely gave me the life lesson and perspectives I needed before his own life ended.

Strength—Because even in a weakened state, he did everything to stay awake and alert to continue our conversations.

During his final days, Samuel called me to his room to tell me that he had been holding onto years of unexpressed feelings that ranged from A to Z throughout his life. Going through some of the, shall we say, "less than stellar events of my life," he used his professorial voice to say, "Now that I am at the end, what (the emotions) I held onto was worthless, David… whatever you feel, express it and get it out of you."

I gave him a whimsical smile, which he immediately (and correctly) read and responded: "Now, don't be a jerk about it."

Samuel addressed one of my most significant weaknesses: saying the first thing that enters my mouth. Whether it was an expression of love, disappointment, sadness, happiness, or another emotion, he urged me to struggle and learn how to communicate my feelings properly. He explained that if I mastered this ability, a clear line of communication would be established, freeing people to walk/work with me or walk away from me. He added that a clear line of communication didn't always translate into a pain-free environment, but while it won't 'stop the hurt" of living, it would "help with the healing" of life.

As my father's condition worsened, my family agreed to take turns staying with him. After my shift ended, I exhaustedly drove home with only thoughts of rest filling my head. As I approached my house, I could see two figures standing on my doorstep and groaned, believing that there was no hospitable energy within me.

A great sense of relief came over me, though, when I recognized one of the people standing on my porch and knew he was well aware of the gravity of my father's situation. We didn't say much because we didn't have to.

"Get some sleep. I'll answer the phone and take care of things," he said.

As I opened the door, I told him it would be a significant load off my mind. But, as we entered the house, he stopped me and said," Wait a sec, y'all still have cable, right?"

"Yeah, we got cable," I said with a smile.

"Cool, then we are going to be here all night."

The man on the porch joking about cable television, was Kevin Bowser, one half of "the twins," as I referred to them. He and his twin brother, Kelvin were good friends of my family and grew up one block away from me. Even though I was ten years younger, nothing could stop this friendship from blossoming. With no brothers of my own, and without any boys my age living on my block, I was relentlessly turning them into the brothers I always wanted.

"The Twins" had very distinct personality traits. Kelvin was more talkative and cocky, while Kevin was more deliberate. But both men were very driven toward their pursuits and motivated in helping guide me through life. I could say so much more about my relationship with the twins collectively, and specifically about my friendship with Kevin. But, the bottom line was this was no ordinary man joking about cable TV at my door—this man was family and Kevin was my brother.

I went to bed, but sleep didn't come easy during that time because I always felt trapped: entangled in the present yet unable to run back into the past when my dad was healthy and very fearful of my future without him. I was perpetually tired but now things were different with Kevin covering the house. I found myself able to comfortably turn off the lights and sleep peacefully for a few hours.

Later that night, light filled the room. Kevin was standing in front of me with the phone in his hand. Because I trusted that Kevin would not wake me for anything minor, I knew who was on the phone and what was going to be said.

"I don't want it," I said.

Holding back tears, Kevin calmly said, "You have to take it."

I don't recall all that was said, but I clearly remember my mother saying two words: "It's time."

As the thoughts of my father's final moments, last breaths, and visions seized me, I moved like a dog chasing his tail, going everywhere but nowhere. I eventually reached my front door but couldn't find my car keys and broke down crying. Kevin stepped up to hug and weep with me while repeating the words, "I know, I know."

Kevin wasn't reiterating empty platitudes; his mother had passed away from cancer two years earlier, and he knew how time and life could slip away, even when you held tightly. The understanding and brotherhood within Kevin's embrace calmed, strengthened, and centered me for my next moments of speeding to the hospital.

I remember running two lights on the way and getting off the elevator to see my mother's and sister's faces in the hallway. I remember entering my father's room. I remember him being dead but still able to feel his presence as I sat alone with him one last time.

Daddy was dead. Mr. Sam was gone.

I was already sorely missing Samuel.

I am incredibly fortunate to have known each of these individuals all wrapped up into one marvelous man. Each incarnation of my father imparted lessons and nuggets of wisdom on me that continually challenged me to move toward my highest potential.

In his eulogy, I wrote about my father's ubiquitous presence even jokingly imitating how he used to yell my name. I acknowledged my fortune at having a good father when others had none. Instead of stating that I didn't know where I would be without him, I admitted to everyone in the church that my father was gone, and I now had to grow up.

My parents always valued a person who honored their word, so I made a vow to be a more compassionate being to those less fortunate and become a "living monument" to my father. I pledged this to my family and friends, knowing that they would never forget and always hold me accountable.

The day I stood on my feet to walk from pew to the pulpit to make this speech,

I ultimately began my journey to becoming a man.'

Both Kevin and Kelvin were pallbearers at my father's funeral, and both helped me get through those initial days by merely being there to listen to me cry.

My relationship and respect for Kevin had grown a great deal during my father's last months. He lived in Philadelphia but worked 90 miles away in New York City at the World Trade Center. Thus his daily commute called for him to catch a train by 7:00 a.m., and despite this, he often opted to come straight to our home to visit my father after working a full day. Because my father's radiation treatments left him depleted of energy, many of Kevin's visits consisted of him just sitting next to Daddy, or doing small things around the house that we were too busy to do. But regardless of what Kevin did, he would always find me before leaving the house to urge me to talk about how I felt.

Our fathers were contemporaries, and although I found Kevin's care and concern vital, I was also intrigued by his attention to my father and our family. Kevin shared that my father was going to be the first friend that he knew he was going to lose and that, "Until I figure out where to be, I would just like to be here."

After losing a parent to cancer, he was all too familiar with the pain and anguish I felt.

Our conversations about my father's treatment were spirited and passionate. While talking, Kevin would speak of alternative healing methods, macro-biotic diets, and how each treatment would ultimately affect the quality of my father's life.

Those talks were tangential strands of discussions that began around 1979 when Kevin decided to become vegan. At the time, I was a meaty, meat-eating, high school freshman who was highly influenced by stimulating conversation and an individual's strong willpower. Kevin's sudden switch intrigued me to no end, and while Kevin ate tofu, I ate cheesesteaks. A typical exchange would involve me asking, "Why are you eating that?" and he countered with, "Why are you eating that?"

Since Kevin was older and much more insightful than I, he always had more answers. When I would say that I didn't know something, he would stop talking and tell me to go look it up so we could finish the conversation.

Now, up to this point in my life, everyone I knew always reminded me that no one likes a dumb or lazy person. Kevin was no different. He bluntly told me that I could not hang around him anymore if I were either. So, not to seem stupid or lazy and to hang around my "big brother," I looked up whatever Kevin and I were discussing.

When I came back with the answer or at least more information, Kevin knew he had me hooked. No matter how long it took for me to look something up, Kevin was willing to pick up the conversation right where we left off. At that point, we would have another conversation—a higher, intellectually informed conversation—that always went well beyond what one ate and how one thought, acted, voted, trained, and lived.

Looking back on it, I am amazed at how much information I learned about different thought processes surrounding various disciplines while really only interested in learning more about Kevin's strong self-discipline toward veganism. The sheer volume of knowledge exchanged between us changed my life's trajectory.

Whenever something is weighing on my mind, I get up early and ride my bicycle to the rising sun, something about it calms me. Something about it calms me. On one of those morning rides, I saw Kevin running across the street toward the train station and rode up to him. Before I could even say anything, he read my facial expression and asked what was wrong with me.

I got off my bike to walk with him into the station, and the more I talked, the more Kevin heard, and the more he heard, the more Kevin slowed down. I was still prattling on as the first call for his train was announced on the PA system. I paused speaking and Kevin put his hand on my shoulder and said, "Screw that train; you're more important. Just relax." Adding, "...but talk fast, because another train is coming in 45 minutes," with a smile.

We didn't solve anything during those 45 minutes and, to be honest, I can't even recall what was so pressing. But, Kevin's attention to my small drama made me remember the moment.

The last time that I spoke to Kevin was Friday, September 7, 2001.

While standing in a market, I heard a familiar voice behind me, saying, "Wheatgrass juice, salad, and water. Man, you are really doing it!" I turned to see Kevin's smiling face, looking in my basket. Amidst a quick chat, he said that he needed my help in getting back in shape.

Our casual conversations throughout our friendship had spurred on my interest in health, fitness, and wellness, and ultimately made me decide to become a personal trainer, so what did I say to Kevin.

"What can I tell you? All I learned was because of you," I said.

He said, "You're training a friend of mine. You spoke at the church of another friend. You're bodybuilding. I hear some real good things about you. You are beyond me now, brother."

Kevin went on to invite me to a barbecue that he was having that Sunday, but I didn't hear all of the details. All I heard was, "You are beyond me now, brother."

These were essentially Kevin's last words to me.

Hearing Kevin, so casually, utter these words was indeed a gift. He had a lot to do with my maturation, and I never thought I could ever go "beyond" him. Hell, I never even wanted to go "beyond" him. His comment was a great moment that was worth acknowledging and extending, but I didn't.

I wanted to hug him but didn't touch him. I wanted to express so much, but my immaturity held me back, and what came out was a bravado-fueled, "Thanks, Dude."

I left the market, telling Kevin that I would see him at his party, but I wanted to say so much more.

As I was driving away, Kevin was leaving the market, and I can still see him. Wearing sandals, a pair of olive green shorts, and a crisp tucked-in white t-shirt, he walked smiling at everyone and no one. I stopped the car and wanted to get out to yell "THANK YOU emphatically!" but didn't.

Instead, I drove off thinking that I would see him later and say it then.

> **Saturday, September 8, 2001**   I never made it to see him because I got caught up in my day and planned to talk to him later.
>
> **Sunday, September 9, 2001** Kevin's party was that day, but I opted to watch football at a sports bar with some friends.
>
> **Monday, September 10, 2001**   Kevin took the day off work while I went for a bike ride and pedaled past his house but felt that I was too sweaty to visit.
>
> **Tuesday, September 11, 2001**   I canceled my day's appointments and elected to go for a long bicycle ride. Kevin went to work early on the 98th floor at the World Trade Center.

I am not going to write any more about my memories because it was awful for everyone.

I had a chance to do and say something so simple, so appropriate, so human, so necessary, and so natural, and my opportunity was taken away in an instant.

I blew it.

Kevin's memorial service was so crowded I resigned myself to the fact that I wasn't going to get in. That's when one of Kevin's friends called my name and said, "You belong in there. Take my spot."

The sight of Kevin's friends, many of whom I had looked up to my whole life, was surreal. 'There they were, standing lifeless like marionettes with lax strings. Many people from Kevin's life stepped up to the podium to speak of his genuine acts of kindness, and I thought, 'He did that for me too.'

It was then that I redefined the word "extraordinary" in my head.

Being extraordinary is not the performance of superhuman acts; it is the action of performing very human acts on a highly consistent and caring level.

Samuel Sylvester and Kevin Bowser were both extraordinary individuals and they changed my life.

The Apology Tour

North America. 2002

"Who would you apologize to, Dave?" That was the question that started it all.

The query was from Steve, or "Padre" as we called him, on my first bike trip across the US. We named Steve "Padre" because while the rest of us were just pedaling across the nation, he was biking to a higher calling.

By ending his trip and then flying directly to seminary at Notre Dame, Steve was literally biking into the priesthood.

Padre stood out to me from the first day of my first bike trip across North America. Maybe because I had just lost my friend on 9/11 and was searching for my own higher calling, or perhaps because he was the first person I met on tour, or maybe something else, but he did stand out.

While most people on tour asked surface questions like "Where did you grow up?" or, "What college did you attend?", Steve's conversations veered toward a more profound and more provocative vein. On the tour's first day, he asked me what I sincerely hoped to accomplish with my ride across the US, and was this going to be my only trip.

I fumbled for a clear and concise answer that never quite appeared, but that didn't seem to bother Padre. He just seemed to love the conversation and to hear people's thought processes. I did too, so I decided to bike with him as much as possible and yap the miles away.

On this sunny day, Steve and I biked along, talking about nothing much until he asked who I would apologize to if I had the opportunity.

Trying to be quick with an answer, I replied that I'd been rude to one of the other riders in the food line. But Steve cut me off right away and snapped, "C'mon, Dave—dig deeper.

Even though I barely knew Steve, something commanding in his voice made me respond immediately to "dig deeper," just as he asked.

As I began to unearth my life's various interactions mentally, we rode abreast on the road, saying nothing, with only the whir of our wheels breaking the silence.

Once I thought of someone, I began to share the story until a light rain stopped me. I tried speaking again, but a severe weather system that dropped the temperature darkened the skies and unleashed torrents of rain changing everything.

The sudden condition change decreased visibility and forced Steve, and I to now ride in a single file.

As my glasses fogged up, I found myself slowing down even more and only paying attention to what was directly in front of my wheel. Now cocooned in my apologetic memories by the rainy day's end, I had a list of people that I could/should apologize to.

The next day, I approached Steve with my list—and before I could even begin, he cut me off: "Why are you talking to me? Why aren't you speaking to them?"

"Yeah, that's another great question," I thought.

Why wasn't I talking to these people? I thought about the answer to that all day.

It took bicycling 70 miles to conclude that I needed to apologize to people, but it took biking another 800 miles or so over the next weeks to finally work up the nerve to say, "I'm sorry."

Now, apologies are tricky because it isn't enough just to say, "I'm sorry." To get the apology right, you have to explain what you did and why you did it, and THEN say that you're sorry.

From that point, the person receiving the apology can make three choices:

- Accept your apology.
- Say, "I don't accept your apology."
- Say, "Screw you."

I am not gonna lie: the first call was tough to make, but after I did it, I felt lighter and cleaner. It was a cathartic moment that left me wanting to make more calls.

In making these calls, I experienced all of the potential answers, but I didn't care. I was freed emotionally.

After apologizing to one friend, he remained speechless for a few moments then said, "Man, I don't even remember that shit."

"Yeah, but I do."

My friend asked me what was happening to me on this tour and I said that I couldn't explain it, "but I kinda like it."

Me too," he said and added, "See you when you get home, brother."

So now that you've read my story, I ask:

Who would you apologize to?
Furthermore, what's stopping you?

Lemonade, That Cool Refreshing Drink

The Wisconsin Dells, Wisconsin. 2002

Even though I've bicycled across Africa, Asia, Australia, North America twice, and around Philadelphia countless times, I don't take myself too seriously as a cyclist.

Never was that more evident than when I was bicycling across the United States in 2002 and decided not to strive to be the first one to finish, but rather be DFL.

Dead Fucking Last.

Why??...Boredom, mostly.

Each day, every touring rider was getting better conditioned, and by the time we pedaled from Oregon to Wisconsin, we were peaking. I knew this when the tour organizers said that the day's ride would be a flat and fast 97 miles, many of us assuredly said, "No problem."

Now finishing DFL wasn't going to be an easy task because we would have to go slower than Larry; a very kind 66-year-old bicyclist who found everything of interest and frequently stopped to investigate it thoroughly.

Knowing this, my friends; Scott, Steve, and I created a simple plan: Stop Everywhere.

Our 97-mile day began with us biking until we stopped at a park to watch a Little League game from every vantage point.

We watched the game with the parents in the stands for one inning, sat in one team's dugout for an inning, and switched dugouts to cheer for the other team for another inning. Then we high5'd both sides and pedaled away.

Biking slowly and stopping everywhere, was pretty much how our day progressed, until lunchtime.

With Wisconsin being known for its bratwurst, around 11 AM, we decided to find the best brats along our route. Our search was fun and took us to two pretty good places, but the third was the most interesting.

While in a store, I asked a guy who had the best brats, and he proclaimed that his homemade brats were the best and was willing to fire up his grill to prove it.

"Okay," we said.

As it turned out, the guy was the manager of a nearby railroad museum, and he did, indeed, fire up his grill to fix us some brats in front of an old train right outside of the museum. His brats were pretty tasty.

Our day of frequent stops and starts was enjoyable, but it was getting late and time to speed through the remaining 20 miles of our cycling day.

To effciently pedal, we formed a paceline—where everyone rides close together in a single-file so that the lead cyclist "breaks the wind," helping others save energy by riding in the wake. Although I'm not fond of them, pacelines are effcient.

While taking my turn breaking the wind, I saw a woman jogging and decided to slow down to her pace and talk. Like most people we met that day, she was very interested in where we were going and why and we began a conversation.

I thought our chat was great until she said, "K"—not even a full "Okay"—and ran into a clearing on her right. Her goodbye was so awkward and perplexing that I jokingly shouted, "White folks can be weird. "To which my friend Scott chuckled and replied, "Yeah, they can be."

We laughed as we pedaled up a slight hill and made a right, and continued to bike up a low, sloping, straight tree-lined county road. As we biked, we couldn't help but notice two people ahead of us, standing on the roadside.

With each pedal stroke, the figures became clearer, and we could see that they were children. It seemed odd, but what did I know. Once we were within 20 yards away and within earshot, we could now see a boy and girl excitedly jumping up and down, holding a cardboard sign that said "GO BIKERS!" with three balloons attached to it.

"STOP! STOP! STOP!" they screamed.

We stopped and noticed a small kid's table with a pitcher of lemonade and some plastic cups on it. Assuming that they had seen the other cyclists throughout the day, we obliged the kids and had some lemonade and made small talk. Now, there is only so much small-talk that you can make with a kid before "Law & Order SVU" rolls up asking why you are speaking to a child, so after another few moments, we said that we had to go—which prompted a very whiny, "You can't go" in response.

"Why?" Scott asked.

That's when we heard a female voice yell from the porch, "Because the cookies aren't done yet!"

We looked up to see the woman who had been running with us earlier. She explained that she was so abrupt with her "K" departure because we'd helped her run faster, and she reached the shortcut much sooner than expected.

She went on to say that our individual stories touched her. She explained the balloons were left over from her mother's birthday party the night before, and her siblings made the sign.

As we sat on the porch chatting with her family, the young woman said she, "just got caught up in our conversation and wanted to do something good… And who doesn't like cookies?"

We enjoyed their warmth and hospitality but it was soon time for us to make our own abrupt "K" departure and push on. As we biked along, we spoke about how cookies, conversation, and lemonade did a lot for our energy and of the randomness of what just happened. I believe that Scott summed it up best by saying, "If we were going fast, we would have blown right by it all."

It was just getting dark by the time we reached our hotel, but our day wasn't complete. Our cycling odometers read 98 miles, and we decided to bike around for an additional two to reach an even 100. Then, it is complete.

We high5'd each other as we coasted into the hotel parking lot as if we'd just won the Tour d' France, confidently yelling, "Dead Fuckin' Last!" But our exuberance was short-lived as the bike tour leader approached us and asked, "Have you guys seen Larry?"

Oh well, Almost Dead Fuckin' Last wasn't so bad either.

Time For My
Fat Ass to Pay

The Ethiopian Mountains. 2004

"Either way, you are going to pay."

That was how one Ethiopian rider described how I would deal with the rampant begging that I would encounter in his country.

Mostly kids but sometimes adults, the begging scenario was always the same: Someone would approach you smacking their open palm, yelling, "You! You! You, give me money."

From that point on, I had two options:

I could "pay" by giving them some money.

Or, I could elect not to give them money, and "pay" having to listen to whatever insults they chose to hurl my way. I know what you are thinking: "Screw that—how bad can a joke be?"

Pretty bad.

To illustrate my point, one day I was riding with a woman cyclist, and the beggars asked her for some money. When she refused, the man pointed and yelled, "Youuuuuuuu! You are so ugly. You will never be married. You and your ugliness will grow old and die—alone!" I told you that it could get pretty bad. It was as if the nation read nothing but joke books on how to harshly roast people.

Back to my story, I was biking up a very steep Ethiopian mountain and not going fast at all. In fact, I was going so slow that three kids were actually jogging with me. Sweat poured off me with each turn of the pedal while the kids, who were used to the surroundings, just smiled and ran around me like it was nothing.

The kids' smiles were so bright that they momentarily lightened my mood as I slogged up the mountain, but that moment was brief. Soon, the ringleader jogged ahead and turned around so he could backpedal and look me in the eye. He stopped smiling and yelled, "You! You! You—give me money."

Painfully I grunted, "Man, I ain't got no money." Immediately, all of the kids stopped smiling and jogging. Now, it was time for me to pay.

The ringleader yelled, "Youuuuuuuuuuuuuuuuuu! You—are too fat for these hills."

Even though the joked was hurled at me, I found it kind of funny and snickered a bit. I braked hard and wheeled around to glare at the kids, who were now 20 yards or so downhill.

Thinking that I might pedal down the mountain after them, two kids had a bit of fear in their eyes, but the ringleader, who was standing between them, looked at me fearlessly. Then, extending his arms to touch his friends' shoulders, he sucked his teeth and then glanced at his friends as if to say, "Relax, his fat ass ain't biking downhill to get us."

And you know what? He was right.

All I could do was breathlessly mutter, "If I could catch you..." under my breath.

Power

Iringa, Tanzania. 2005

Plato said: "The measure of a man is what he does with power."

Admittedly, I never devoted much thought to the philosophical concept of "power" or its usage until I realized that I had some.

I enjoyed a rare day off of my cycling trip across Africa by hanging out with some Peace Corps volunteers I met. After a day/evening of partying, I decided that it was time to make my way back to camp and almost immediately regretted the decision.

Within thirty minutes of stumbling through Tanzania's rural and dark streets, I found myself way too lost to make my way back to my campsite. I needed help and entered the only nearby building with some lights on.

Upon entering, I saw that it was a dimly lit bar with only four people inside. One man was behind the bar fixing a drink; another man was leaning on the bar with a woman kissing his neck and one man who was drunk asleep in the corner.

I never moved from the doorway and shouted into the room if there was any place where I could get a cab. The man behind the bar pointed to the guy passed out in the corner and laughed as he said, "He's a cab driver."

"Fuck that!! I'll walk," I said and turned to leave.

"Wait, are you American?" the guy behind the bar asked.

When I said, "yes," the man introduced himself as Peter and asked where I was going.

While shaking hands, I said my campsite's name, and he said that he'd drive me there if I drank with him. "I don't like drinking alone," Peter said.

We chatted about my reasons for bicycling across Africa over that drink, but the conversation turned a bit by the time we sipped our second.

It was very apparent that Peter knew a great deal about American culture and wanted my opinion on what was happening in the US, as a black American. Soon the questions came flying out: "Do the police target black men? What did I think of the Kobe Bryant case? Could a black man get a fair shot in America?"

With barely any time to respond and feeling the effects of a day's worth of drinking, I cut him off and flatly stated, "Ya know. I think that we each are the main architects in our rise and demise."

Peter stopped talking to put his drink down and stared at me for a moment. "That's, that's sensible….why don't I hear that in the news?"

"How would I know," I said with a smirk. I tried changing the subject, but Peter wasn't going to let me.

What's America's biggest export?? he asked.

"Cars," I said dismissively.

"No!! It's entertainment!!" he snapped.

Then, citing Iringa's rise in violence against women and senior citizens, he railed on about "American entertainment," affecting his countrymen's minds, ideas, and actions.

"We didn't have that shit before!! Now, it's common." He angrily said, adding, "these fools are bragging and telling people how to commit crimes."

"How many people can you kill on a record!!!?? What are you giving us?!!," he yelled.

Usually, I don't particularly appreciate being yelled at, but felt that Peter's points had some validity. He continued by saying that in the songs of his youth, artists lyrically stated that the only thing worth fighting for was a societal wrong and that the only thing worth dying for was an injustice.

He tried singing the Five Stairsteps hit lyric, "Ooh Child things will get easier" But then abruptly stopped singing to yell, "But this shit…this shit is craziness. You rap about going to get big money, big rims, big titties, big sex and all kinds of big shit, and after all of that gettin', you *still* have a shitty day and are *STILL* angry. I don't get it."

It was evident that Peter had been storing up his ire for any American who walked through his door, and today I was the lucky one. He had unloaded his feelings with such ferocity that his eyes were now slightly bulging and needed to pause for a few moments. I sat there with my mouth shut, and my mind open, thinking about his observations on rap lyrics.

After some moments of silence, he blurted, "And why the fuck should I drink Sprite?!"

Knowing that Sprite is a sponsor of the NBA and some hip-hop artists, I used this as an opportunity to be a smart ass and break the mood a bit. "Because that shit is good?" I said.

Even Peter had to smile at that one.

"It actually is," he said with a chuckle. But he quickly got serious again and said he held me responsible for doing something to "change the world."

Incredulous, I looked at him and asked what he expected me to do. "I'm just a mother fuckin' biker in here with your drunk ass," I said.

Peter shook his head and said, "No. No. No," and pointed his finger at me. He said, "You are more. You told me that you have no money, and I believe you. But somehow, with nothing, you managed to figure it out here," he said, pointing to his heart. "And here," pointing to his head. "To get here," Peter pointed to the ground. "Then, you have power, and you just have to figure out how to use it."

"Wow," I thought; no one had ever said anything like that to me before.

Peter's statement, "You have power, you just have to figure out how to use it," was his 'drop the mic' moment, and he knew it.

He also knew not to over-talk the moment and began cleaning things around the bar, eventually going to the storeroom, and leaving me to sit in silence and let the wisdom of his words sink in.

He returned a few minutes later and, now, with everything off his chest, guzzled the rest of his drink, slammed the glass down, and loudly said, "let's go!!"

On the ride to my camp, two points became very apparent to me:

- I would NEVER have made it home by myself.
- Peter was now a different person.

There were no provocative questions or serious undertones; there was only laughter on our drive.

When we reached my darkened campsite, Peter honked the horn for a while as I exited his car and screamed, "Dave's home!!" into the night air.

Not wanting to wake the cyclists sleeping in their tents, I tried shushing Peter, but he laughed and said, "What?? You should be announced!"

I laughed and leaned in the car and asked if he was ok to drive. He smiled and said, "Shit, I got you here, didn't I??"

"Yeah, you're right," I said.

Peter then got out of the car to shake my hand, and I hugged him instead. As we embraced, I said, "You be safe out there."

"And, you change the world out there," he replied.

Peter then honked the horn as he drove off again, yelling, "Dave's home!!"

I never saw Peter again, but he crosses my mind from time to time, and I wonder what he would think of how I'm using my power now.

Steel is Real

Sudan. 2005

If you read the chapter, "Time For My Fat Ass to Pay," you remember how some Ethiopian beggar kids taunted me when I didn't give them money.

Those kids were just baiting me—but if those same kids had encountered me a few weeks earlier, when I was bicycling through Sudan, they might have had a point. You see, that's when my big ass broke a bike, literally.

With no clouds in the sky and not too much heat, I was cycling south in Sudan towards the city of Al Qadarif.

As pleasant as the atmosphere was, it was in direct contrast to the awful road conditions that had me sliding in the sand in spots and dodging rocks in others.

While I bounced around something fierce and did my best to swerve around some of the rocks, my bike quickly "shifted" to the left slightly and suddenly, I felt a bit of "give" in the ride. Thinking that I had a flat, I stopped and checked both my tires: hard as rocks.

It was all in my head, I thought, but the problem was still there when I began riding again. I decided to give my bike a more thorough inspection. That was when I discovered a big crack in my bike's frame at the rear dropout. "Oh, God, no!" I yelled at my bike. "This can't be happening."

A cracked bike frame is as big a bike issue as you can have. Seeing this meant that I would have to buy another bicycle somehow or worse, fly back home and consider my trip to be over.

I was distraught and needed to calm down.

For about a mile to the next town, I did my best to clear my mind while stepping over rocks and schlepping my body and bike through the sand and dirt streets. But, I guess I didn't do enough because I was still just as heated emotionally.

After getting a cold soda from a souk, I sat outside, staring at my frame's crack, weighing the scenarios of returning home or buying another bicycle. Both of these options required money I didn't have and angered the hell out of me. By now, other cyclists had joined me in getting a cold drink, but I was wrapped up in my problems and unaware of their presence.

They were also unaware of my bike issues. "SHIT!" I yelled and kicked my bike.

My outburst startled the other cyclists, and as they went to pick up my bike, they said, "Hey Dave, your bike's broken."

"No shit," I growled.

"What are you going to do? Go home? Fly in another bike from the States?"

"How the fuck do I know?" I continued growling.

Another rider rolled up, looked at my bike, and right away said, "Hey Big Dave, your frame is cracked."

"Thanks, genius."

This was not my finest hour.

Then Midhat, the tour's Sudanese guide, biked up and looked at my bike. I was waiting for him to point out the obvious as the others had, but he didn't.

Instead, he knocked on the frame and asked, "What is that?"

"It's steel," I said.

"No problem." Midhat said assuredly.

What?? Without even addressing me, just focusing only on the problem, he proudly thumped his chest and proclaimed, "Relax. We can fix anything. See you at camp," and jumped on his bike.

The walk to our camp was another few miles where Midhat was anxiously waiting.

"No time, let's go," he said.

"Where are we going?" I asked

"To fix," he said, patting my back.

Clueless as to what Midhat's plan was, I asked how/where we were going.

"We're getting a ride," he said.

"Uhh, OK," I thought.

As we walked towards the main road, my friend and fellow rider, Brian ran up to hug me and put some money in my hand.

"Calm down, big fella, I don't know where you're going, but you're gonna need some cash."

"Thanks, man. I don't know where I am going, either."

Midhat spoke with such assurance that I expected a truck to be waiting at the main road, but there wasn't.

Instead, we waited at the main road...for a passing truck.

We flagged down the truck and hopped on the back to ride a few miles to a garage in another town. Midhat entered first, leaving me to stand outside, holding my bike frame and emerged moments later with a man wearing green overalls and clutching a blowtorch.

What happened next was nothing to the man in the overalls, but it was everything to me because it saved me thousands of dollars in either purchasing a new bike or flying home. Sensing my anxiety, the man in the overalls placed his hand on my shoulder to say, "calm down, dude," and then lit a cigarette with his blowtorch.

Within minutes, he completed the ugliest weld in the world, and my plans to bicycle to South Africa were back on.

If my frame was aluminum, carbon fiber, or any other material, there was no way I could have gotten a weld. But, as Midhat proclaimed, "Steel, it is real."

And here is the best part: when it came time to pay, the welder only wanted six bucks!

He saved my trip, so I gave him much more, but what a bargain! I hugged everyone in the shop except for the welder. He wasn't a hugger and held up his unlit blowtorch to stop me when I went in for an embrace.

And, that's the story.

I didn't have any more bike issues on my trip—until I cracked my front fork in Kenya. Oh wait, I forgot that I also cracked my seat post bolt at least 12 times on this tour and ended up riding almost 100 miles standing up because of it.

And those were all of my bike issues in Africa.

Hmm, now that I think about it, maybe that Ethiopian kid was right. Maybe my ass was too fat for those hills.

People Are Dying

Botswana. 2004

They say that, "seeing is believing."

But there are also those unique times when someone needs to tell you exactly what you are looking at, so you truly see and comprehend it all.

That was the case when I was bicycling through Botswana.

Before I continue, let me say that I loved Botswana. As a large cyclist who likes sprinting and just spent months pedaling up and down mountains through almost every weather condition that one can think of, I looked forward to Botswana's sunny skies and flat paved roads.

The country was also devoid of people. The population was so small that one day I remarked to another cyclist, "What if they built a country and nobody came?"

But I didn't overthink it. I just knew that without too many people to encounter and nothing but flat and fast roads, Botswana was my own personal "Promised Land."

Almost every day in Botswana, I saw more elephants than people and while it was beautiful to see these majestic creatures just roaming free, it did pique my curiosity as to why. When I came back home, I read that many elephants are naturally migrating to the region and taking refuge in the country. However, no one knows why.

As for the nation's small human population, people know why: AIDS.

The spread of AIDS had reached epidemic proportions. One in four people have contracted the disease, devastating the population to the point that there are now less than four people per square mile. It's an amazingly sad statistic that affects every aspect of the country, and where I observed it most was in commerce.

I had pedaled through many small towns and villages throughout Africa and saw a lot of open-air markets and bazaars that were full of merchants competing for business. But in Botswana, I saw only a few people and only one of everything else: One market. One butcher. One general store. One hardware store. One school. Even one clothing store.

Although I saw this, nothing about it struck me as odd until I was drinking a soda outside of a village's lone general store. While sipping the day away, I noticed two casket makers directly across the road from each other.

"Hmmm," I thought. Then, I stopped a local man walking past me. "Excuse me, why are there two casket companies here?" I asked.

Looking at the two businesses and then at me, he flatly said, "People are dying, brother," and walked into the store.

There it was, plain and straightforward: casket makers were the only industry vibrant enough for competition. Everything about Botswana and its empty sunny streets came into a new focus for me. All of a sudden, I didn't believe this place to be so heavenly anymore.

In Blue-and-White

Too Many Places.

My friend, Professor Maurice Baynard once said, "What you have to teach the world lies somewhere amid the challenges you have faced in it."

That said, this chapter is about my challenging encounters with Niggers on my travels.

That's right, I said it, Niggers.

My first encounter was when I was in Lilongwe, Malawi, bicycling Africa, and some other cyclists said they saw a store named Niggers.

Initially, when the other riders, who were all white, informed me of this, I thought it was a terrible joke. But after noticing how they were waiting for my reaction, I knew they weren't.

As we walked to the store, I held onto the hope that maybe this was a mistake, and perhaps it was a store run by a bunch of over-bearing mothers-in-laws called "Naggers."

But upon seeing the blue tent with white letters spelling out the word, I thought, "This shit is real."

I tried walking ahead of my friends in a feeble attempt to escape them, but they kept pace.

I wanted to yell, "Yo!!!! This shit is embarrassing; clean it up," but said nothing and just kept marching.

My eyes were practically bulging out of my head by the time I reached the store, and when I saw that one of the men working was asleep, I mentally screamed, "Jesus Christ, dude!! Are you going to live down to every stereotype??"

The store sold their version of hip-hop-style clothing, and in trying not to draw attention to the conversation, I practically whispered, "What's up with the name?"

After hearing my distinct non-Malawian accent and deducing that I was from America, one man thumped his chest and proudly proclaimed, "P-Diddy New York City! we're the niggers!!!"

"Goddammit!" I thought.

Here I was, honoring a fellow black man by cycling across the "Mother-Land," and THIS is how some brothers greet me: P-Diddy New York City! We're the niggers!?!

My first reaction was to laugh because that is how I handle many things, but this wasn't funny at all. It was pathetic. I wanted to have a conversation with these guys but didn't because I needed to have a serious talk with myself first.

I grabbed something to eat but walked back past later on and watched the guys smiling and selling their products. I thought, "How can I blame them for calling their store 'Niggers'?"

I didn't physically write Niggers on that tent but certainly said the word with impunity when I was younger and engaged in the debate on using the word.

I argued that it didn't matter because it was just "one word' that was a part of a song or a movie or some other form of entertainment. I also rationalized that the difference was all within the spelling: nigger vs. nigga.

But as I stood in this dusty Lilongwe street, with some P-Diddy songs on my iPod, the irony of the situation hit me: "I paid for the image of Niggers to be exported out into the world.

It was very apparent that I supported a negative image of black men, treating it as nothing more than an ember of exported entertainment. But, that ember made its way around the planet to become a raging fire that now engulfed and defined me.

The chickens had indeed returned home to roost, and these guys weren't the problem; I was.

I was trying to be a positive black man, but all they saw when they looked at me was a nigger. But of even more significance, a nigger is what they see when they looked upon themselves.

Some people will see the picture of the store and laugh when hearing about this, downplaying it as just an isolated occurrence; it wasn't.

Two years later, when I bicycled from Istanbul to Beijing, I got my haircut in a Tajikistan barbershop where most of the staff called me a "Beeg Neegah!"

I left the shop, not wanting to believe what happened, but as I looked and saw some kids with 50 Cent T-shirts, I knew it was all too real.

I was also called a Nigger...endearingly...by a taxi driver in Azerbaijan, some guys in Kenya, two Australian guys, and some Dutch rappers in the Netherlands.

In Chicago, I spoke with a young rapper who said he got my point but argued that he would still use the word because of its versatility. "A lot of shit rhymes with it," he said.

We chuckled about many of the ways "nigger" could be used and rhymed, but after our laughter subsided, I said, "you're right, but maybe we shouldn't hear those verses anymore."

Each reader will do what they are going to do concerning further usage of this word.

But for those who continue to use the word, I will ask, at what point in a black boy's life is he supposed to look in the mirror and no longer see a nigger but instead gaze upon a black man??

Is there a "black-mitzvah" ceremony or something?

I joke because I've made up my mind on using the word and will not argue or preach to anyone about how they look or call upon themselves: I just lay out things, as I saw them, in blue-and-white.

Catch me, Big Man!

Cape Town, South Africa. 2005

After beginning in Cairo, Egypt and cycling for almost five months through Sudan, Ethiopia, Kenya, Tanzania, Malawi, Zambia, Botswana and Namibia, we had finally reached our destination of Cape Town, South Africa.

We began the day pedaling slowly in one giant paceline, but as we got closer, we quickened our pace. By the time we could see the party tents set up for us, offiicially marking the end of our tour, we were pretty much sprinting on our bikes. Once in the park, we threw our bikes down to grab champagne glasses and then basked in the unique thrill of achievement.

Even though we were all sore, dirty, hungry, sunburnt, a lot skinnier and exhausted, there was no containing our delight as we laughed, cried, hugged, and joyfully yelled at each other.

Even with help from a thesaurus, I still can't quite find the exact words to describe my moment but I honestly believe that this picture captures it all.

Bart, a Dutch cyclist, had hugged almost every rider except for me, and when we locked eyes, he yelled, "Catch me, Big Man!!"

Before I could even react, Bart threw his champagne down, began sprinting towards me, and leaped at me. I had no choice but to catch him along with all of the beautiful emotions embodied within him. "I can't believe it, brother," he said. "Neither can I," I said with tears streaming down my face, "...neither can I."

I love this picture.

Badge

Uzbekistan-Tajikistan border. 2007

After wrapping up my Uzbekistan-Tajikistan border crossing on my Istanbul to Beijing bicycle trip, I hung around the border control offiice to waste time with the agents. We were having a great time, too, until this one man sauntered in. I had no clue who he was, but I knew that he was a boss from how everyone snapped to attention. Upon entering, it was as if the air itself changed—there was no more laughter, hats weren't askew anymore, and the music had been turned off.

The room's "temperature change" was so abrupt that *I* even sat up straight.

Always being one to take chances, I asked the man who he was, and he casually pulled out his badge and said his title. Because of his accent, I didn't quite understand him but noticed that he lit up when I said, "So, you are THE MAN in these parts."

With a heavy smoker's gravel, he slowly said, "YES, I am The Man."

I smiled and told him that since he was "The Man," he should pull out his badge with much more flair. What I actually said was something closer to "Dude!! If I had a badge, I would be pulling it out like this!" I then proceeded to act like my passport was a badge and began flipping it open like they did in

57

70's and 80's TV cop shows yelling "BAM" each time I did.

After a few harsh critiques of his 'flair-BAM' technique, "The Man" tossed me his badge and coolly said: "Show me."

That's all it took for me to begin walking all around the border offiice and "BAM-ing" everyone—each instance being more comical than the other and getting crazy laughter. At one point, I slid on the floor and produced the badge with a loud, "Bam!!"

I was getting so many laughs that when I motioned towards the door and wasn't stopped, I stepped outside.

Once out of the offiice, I put my newfound powers to the test and stopped a car. That's right: with just my bike gear on, I walked into the street, flipped my badge, yelled "BAM," and stopped a car.

The driver came to an abrupt stop and then looked completely confused as I barked for him to "slow down" with an American accent.

After a few seconds, I stepped back and told the driver to "move on," but the car didn't budge.

It was then I realized that the driver might have been listening to me, but he wasn't looking at me at all. He was instead looking off to my right. When I turned my head in that direction, I saw The Man standing there with a steely "don't you dare move that car" gaze fixated on the driver.

It was only when The Man smiled and gave the driver the subtlest of nods, that the car was put into gear and drove off.

And just like that, I realized I might have been holding the badge, but had none of the power that goes with it: My Playtime was officially over.

I carefully placed the badge back in his hand, said thank you, hugged him, and bicycled on my way.

Poop-arazzi

Rural China. 2007

The possibilities of what I might see and learn within the cultures, terrain, and people of Turkey, Georgia, Azerbaijan, Turkmenistan, Uzbekistan, Tajikistan, Kyrgyzstan, and China had me eager to go on my Istanbul–to–Beijing bicycle tour.

But a lot of the people I encountered were eager to meet me for just one reason: my skin color.

Many of the people, especially in the rural areas, hadn't seen a black person in the flesh, so there were many times where everything would stop just from my walking into a room or across the street. Most times it wasn't a bother, but one time it got to me.

It was when a night soil truck drove next to me.

What is a night soil truck—you ask? If you look in the dictionary, you will see that night soil is human excrement—collected at night from buckets, cesspools, and outhouses—that will be used as manure to fertilize crops.

THAT is night soil.

Now, imagine a truck filled with night soil. Yup, and it smells just like you think it would.

How do I know this?

Well, I was biking with my friend Scott along the rolling hills of Central China, and all of a sudden, the air became putrefied. It was as if a stinky storm cloud rolled in and just got more intense by the second.

I looked at Scott and asked, "Damn, son, did you fart?"

He looked at me and said, "No! I was just about to ask you if you shit yourself!"

We both laughed, but there wasn't anything funny about the situation: It stunk. The smell only intensified as we heard the klickity-klacking of a small tanker pulling its way up the hill, and eventually riding beside us.

The truck smelled the way you think it would, and with errant brown stains all over it, it also looked like you'd expect too. The only thing that was out of place were the four smiling guys sitting happily on the truck's bench seat—all holding up their camera phones and taking pictures of me.

Scott and I had to do something, so we slowed down—and so did the truck.

We then sped up—so did the truck. This can't be happening.

Then we tried really slowing down so the truck would move on, but then heard the grinding of gears as the truck crept along to keep pace.

Yes, shit was actually following us, and it was annoying.

Our bicycling game of cat-and-mouse was exerting and made us breathe more heavily, smelling the awful atmosphere on an even deeper level.

We did this a few times until Scott reached a brilliant conclusion.

"Man, I sure am glad they've seen a white person before," he yelled, and with that remark, he stood up on his bike and sprinted ahead of me.

"Shit—literally, shit!" I thought.

Scott's sudden dash left me alone with the "Poop-arazzi" guys, who just laughed as they pointed at Scott pulling away. Figuring that I wasn't going to shake these guys, I conceded to the moment and continued pedaling up the road until I saw a clearing and pointed to it. I stopped there, got off my bike, and let them take all the pictures they wanted.

The four guys—who spoke NO English, poured out of the truck and treated me as if I was a celebrity. And you know what happened next?

More people stopped.

That's right, three more vehicles stopped, and people got out to take pictures.

I felt like I was in that 80's Faberge Organics shampoo commercial where they tell two friends, and so on, and so on, and so on.

After all was said and done, I posed for a ton of pictures, hugged a bunch of dudes, and advanced race relations just a bit.

And, that's how you make the best of a shitty situation ;)

Don't Let The Dog Get Ya

The Kyrgyzstan Mountains.

So there was this one day in the Kyrgyzstan Mountains...don't all good stories begin that way?

I was on my Istanbul–to–Beijing bicycle tour, and we were two miles above sea level, and the altitude was killing me. It was hard to even think about walking to urinate, let alone bike 70 miles, but I was doing it—one goddamned pedal stroke at a time.

As I was riding up this long sloping road, I saw something up ahead in the distance, along the roadside. I was so far away that I figured that it might be a lone calf or some other small animal, but as I continued further up the road, all the possibilities dwindled to my worst fear.

It was a wild dog.

Once I saw this, I stopped maybe 30 or 40 yards from our intersection point. When I did, the dog stopped too. As an experiment, I rode for a few yards and stopped. Much to my dismay, the dog moved and stopped too.

"Shit," I thought, "I am about to be in a real live dogfight."

I looked behind me for another rider to help me develop a plan, but there were none. I looked ahead but could only faintly make out another rider in a lime green jacket, too far away to hear any yell that I might muster. So I held my tongue and energy.

I couldn't go backward.

There was no going sideways.

It was too cold to stand still.

I could only go forward.

I decided to continue up the road at a slow and steady pace, bracing my body for one big sprint once the dog was close, and then dust him. It wasn't much of a plan, but it was all I had. I didn't know if I could pull this off, but I knew that I wasn't weak and had to do something.

I started pedaling up the road, and the dog closed in, slowing and increasing his pace to correlate directly with mine. I thought that maybe all of this was being filmed for a show like "When Animals Attack: The Big Black Man Edition."

But it wasn't; it was real and no joke.

Once we were ten or 15 yards from each other, I could see the dog in detail. The dog was a lean black German Shepherd mix with no collar, grooming, or anything to say that he'd ever been domesticated. Even though it wasn't the most brilliant move, I wanted to see my foe and stared directly into the dog's eyes. I couldn't help it.

His eyes were locked in on me too. When only a few yards from me, he snarled and picked up his pace.

His snarl was like a personal starting gun for me. I stood up on the pedals to make myself seem larger and menacing, let out a yell and started sprinting. My heart pounded, making adrenaline course through my body—but because of the altitude and this being the fourth month of a five-month ride across Asia, a cramping pain coursed through my body with each beat.

Everything began to hurt:

- My forearms ached from gripping the handlebar so hard.
- My calves screamed from the fierce pedaling,
- My back twinged from standing up for the sudden sprint.
- My chest tightened from heaving.
- My core strained from being scared and tensing so much.
- Every part of me burned—It was hell.

My sudden sprint and yell must have startled the dog for a second because a hitch in his gait made him change direction and get right beside me rather than over-run me. Then, with him on my right and directly next to my back wheel, I could see him.

No, let me not lie here: I couldn't see him. At that point, I didn't dare take my eye off the dirt road—the last thing that I needed to do was fall, but my mind imagined his every detail.

In my mind, I could see the breath leave his mouth as he snarled. I could see the hungry look in his eyes, which made the hairs on his neck stand up like coarse bristles of a stiff brush. In my mind, I could see it all. More adrenaline flowed through me, and more pain flowed with it. But just then, something big happened.

No, the dog didn't bite me, but I thought about it—a lot.

In mere moments, I went from wanting to outrun this dog and being in pain to wondering: How bad can a dog bite be?

Can the pain be worse than what I am feeling now?

Can I give up?

Can this pain end?

I never discovered the answers to these questions because I was able to elude the dog. But as my jellied legs slowed to a stop a few yards down the road, I stared at the dog, which trotted off the roadside to wait for a slower unsuspecting cyclist. I wondered about the moment when I wanted to give up. I don't know what kept me pedaling through it. Maybe it was my will, perhaps it was a basic human instinct to survive, perhaps it was something unique and intrinsic to me—or maybe it was just dumb luck.

But, whatever the case, I am glad of it.

I share this story because I recently spoke with a friend battling some "emotional dogs" from their past.

My friend's "dogs" weren't of their doing—they were just an innocent victim of unfortunate crime and "froze" during it.

Their inability to move during the incident continuously haunts them and creates emotional "dog days" that undermine their best efforts to move forward in life. And often, these "dog days" leave them crying and questioning whether they can continue on at all.

I don't know why my friend called me, but I tried helping them out since they did.

I stayed up all night speaking of my encounter with the Kyrgyzstan dog and other instances where I wanted to stop in life but found something within me to go forward.

I gave my life viewpoint that it often takes the same amount of energy, if not more, to retreat and return to our starting point—so we might as well use our power to take a stand and fight to forge ahead towards a brighter moment.

Speaking with my friend made me see how our past "dog days" can haunt us, and our only defense is an armor that is held together by our own sense of self-confidence.

I hung up the phone thinking about my moment when I wondered if the dog's bite was worse than the pain it took to pedal away.

I made it through my moment with the dog; does that make me smart or a fearless guy?

I wanted to quit and yield to it all; does that make me a bitch?

You'll answer those questions as you like.

But what girds me through my own "dog day" battles is remembering that in a dire moment: I acknowledged that I was having a difficult time, thought of a possible solution, formulated a plan, believed in my strength, and then did all that was in my power to move forward.

This is the thought process and practice that generally gets me through life.

This doesn't mean that all of my decisions are correct, not by a long-shot. But confidence is gained with each of my experiences which helps me quickly evolve from any outcome and be even more prepared for my next adventure.

So if you're reading this, don't fear the dog days—we all get 'em.

Instead, be kind to yourself.

Credit yourself for enduring the moments of your past.

Then do like I did in Kyrgyzstan and be beautifully human and evolve to go one more step, moment, and pedal stroke beyond the "dogs' that are nipping at your heels and beyond where you thought your limits were.

If you do, I believe those subsequent battles will be more manageable.

Remember: Don't let the dog get ya!

Cheeseburger—Cheeseburger

The Kyrgyzstan Mountains.

While biking up a Kyrgyzstan mountainside, I came across three kids whose picture I wanted to take. While getting out my camera, the kids asked where I was from. As soon they heard, "America," began performing how they thought Americans behaved.

One girl began smiling with a cheesy grin that took up most of her face and made the peace sign with her fingers.

The boy with the hat just started dancing for no reason, and twirling around and around again.

The kid in the center put his fingers on his eyes to open them more and began droning on and on, "Cheeseburger! Cheeseburger! Want Cheeseburger."

I didn't know what to think after seeing their display, but I was smiling and dancing with them and sure did want a cheeseburger.

Your Kiss Is On My List

Las Cruces, New Mexico. 2008

While volunteering at the Mesilla Valley Hospice in Las Cruces, New Mexico, I delivered lunches and warm smiles to the patients.

I also offered a big hug with each tray of food, and one patient found my hug offer especially delightful.

Her name was Myrtress, and she was adorable.

She was so adorable that I asked this 75-year-old woman if I could give her an extra hug and a kiss. "Ooooh, I'd like that," she cooed.

As I bent down to give Myrtress a peck, her attending nurse stopped me and said that I could not kiss her on the forehead.

"That's my spot," the nurse proudly proclaimed and explained that she gently kissed Myrtress's forehead daily, even if she was sleeping, just to remind Myrtress that she was around.

I complied, but as I leaned over to kiss Myrtress on her cheek, it was apparent that she had other plans.

She smiled as she hugged me friskily and licked my face.

Her wink afterward made everyone laugh and left me smiling.

At the end of my service day, I went back to each patient room to say goodbye, and everyone was sitting up and awake when I stopped by, except for Myrtress.

Myrtress was lying down, and I planned just to walk over and whisper, "Goodbye," but before I could utter a word, an imprint of full lips on her forehead stopped me.

The lipstick mark on Myrtress' forehead said, "It doesn't take much to touch someone's life and even less to make an impact" and was the perfect signature to end a beautiful day.

Even though I had nothing to do with it, that kiss will probably go down as one of my all-time favorites.

You Earned This

Las Cruces, New Mexico. 2009

One of the most bittersweet embraces I ever had occurred in 2009 during my second bicycle journey across North America.

On that ride, I volunteered one day at a different charitable organization each week. The places I gave service to that summer ranged from homeless shelters to addiction centers to schools, a hospice care facility and more.

But, only one charity, The Mesilla Valley Hospice, asked one of my favorite questions, "How many people can you hug in a day?"

"How many ya got?" I replied.

My day at the hospice was a life lesson in different forms of appreciation.

The hospice administrators very professionally greeted me by saying, "thank you for choosing our charity to be a part of your journey."

A custodian who had just clocked out for the day, enthusiastically said, "I couldn't leave without saying: Thank you!"

A chef stopped preparing meals to kiss me on the cheek, take my hand, and pray for my safety as well as bless me with energy to motivate those who I encounter.

Even a groundskeeper took me aside to give me his phone number and said, "Call me if you need anything in New Mexico.

Each person I met at the facility honored me by expressing their appreciation for my actions in a different way and I expressed my thanks by hugging everyone a few moments longer and tighter than I usually do.

I embraced many people that day, but one who stood out was Robert, an 80-year-old patient who'd been told about my travels and was waiting for me when I entered his room.

Visibly excited and moving in a robust manner that belied his age and condition, Robert immediately sat up in his bed and said, "I am so proud to meet you."

Despite an almost 50-year age gap, Robert and I bonded quickly, and he sized me up almost immediately. "Man, you got a look in your eye; I bet trouble just always seemed to find you, didn't it?" he said with a playful wink.

We joked a lot during our time together but focused our conversation on his boldness in dealing with the precious time that he had remaining. He told his doctors "not to bother" when they wanted to amputate his leg, adding, "Look, I know I am gonna die soon...Give me some dignity."

Most people I encounter want to hear about where I have traveled in my lifetime, but not Robert. He said he was already aware of my back-story and wanted to instead speak on where I was going in life because he wasn't going to be alive to see it.

"I see things in you," he said.

Robert was special. I wanted to continue sitting with him but couldn't because of my volunteering duties. However, I did stop by his room before leaving for the day. He was napping when I entered his room but stirred as I began to leave. "Shhhh, go back to sleep, brother. I'm just stopping by to say 'goodbye,'" I quietly said. I extended my hand to shake, but he shook his head and began to get up, adamantly refusing any assistance.

"No!" he loudly barked.

Robert then began to bite his bottom lip and squirm around from side-to- side to get to the bed's edge and sit up in a position to stand. It was a struggle to watch him make this grand gesture of appreciation, but he didn't want any help. He paused for a moment to gather himself and looked up at me and said, "You earned this, man."

Then, by shifting his weight away from his withered leg onto his good one, he finally stood tall. He embraced me with a huge grin and said, "You added another week to my life!"

In a hospice where people die every day, I didn't only hear Robert's words, I felt them and left the Mesilla Valley Hospice feeling honored to have been a part of something so beautiful.

But, that feeling didn't last long.

Four days later, I was cycling through West Texas and took a break to call the hospice and check on Robert and some other patients.

"Robert's gone."

I'm sure the hospice administrator said more, but, "Robert's gone," was all I heard until I hung up. Then, all I heard was my crying.

I appreciate our moment, Robert;
Rest In Peace, Brother.

One Man Can Change the World

Galveston, Texas. 2008

In August 2008, I became the first bicyclist to cross the Galveston Causeway, legally. This crossing, which came with a police escort, news crews, photographers, and other cyclists in tow, happened because of one woman, Zeeyon Walker.

Zeeyon was a Galveston area graduate student who said that I "had to" bike through her city when she heard I was bicycling across the nation for a second time.

"The community needs to see you and is going to love you," she said. Galveston was not originally on my trip route, but Zeeyon was relentless about changing my plans. During one phone conversation, she enthusiastically exclaimed, "When these kids meet a brother who has bicycled across CONTINENTS— it's gonna be something. Dave, you are going to change their lives."

The notion of inspiring another generation had pretty much convinced me to change my plans, but I didn't say 'yes' right away because I needed to figure out a few logistical aspects. Zeeyon must've taken my hesitation as a stall tactic because she said, "if you do come, I will take care of everything; Trust me! The community is gonna love you!!"

"Ok, I'll do it."

Zeeyon didn't lie either and took care of everything. Houston was my stop before Galveston, and she arranged for a few members of a local cycling club to wait for me when I pedaled into town. I was informed that they were going to accompany me along the 70-mile ride into Galveston and also provide a support van for the day.

I was glad to hear this because the forecast the next day was a brutal 90 degrees and 90% humidity. I've now bicycled in all types of conditions, and pedaling in high heat and humidity is pretty much the worst. Your body feels like it is just leaking energy, and you can never drink enough to replace what you've lost in sweat.

On that ride, I remember stopping at a convenience store and guzzling a 32-ounce Gatorade so fast at the counter that the clerk said, "Damn dude!! Can you do that again??"

"Sure can—ring me out for another," I said and guzzled another.

When we reached Galveston and finally saw the causeway, I was ready to pedal across it to get to an air-conditioned hotel room and end the day.

But I couldn't—we had to wait for the police escort.

The wait for the police was awful because there was nowhere shady to sit, which just made me sweatier and crankier by the minute. After about 20 minutes of waiting, I had enough and said, "Fuck it! Let's just ride it."

As soon as I said this, Ron Contreras, one of the cyclists who had been super friendly to me all day, walked over to me and snapped," No!...we are gonna do this right. THIS is not about you right now."

I was clueless about what Ron was talking about when he said, "THIS is not about you right now," but could see a fire in his eyes and backed down. The wait continued to be miserable, but I suffered in silence and didn't dare face Ron's wrath again.

Twenty minutes later, though, our period of waiting and silence was over.

In a blink of an eye, members of a few local bike road/mountain clubs, individual cyclists, police cruisers, the Galveston bike police, and even a few joggers poured into the blacktop area from every possible direction. Even a Galveston city councilman showed up wearing his bike gear. Each person was very excited about biking the causeway—which hadn't been open to cyclists—and thanked me for helping get a bike lane.

I thought "this" must be what Ron was talking about. I didn't have the heart to say I had NO idea I was helping them out and just smiled as I hugged people and said, "your welcome" over and over. It took some more time for people to get organized, but soon Ron was in my face again, this time with a smile and saying, "It's time: lead the way, big man."

I remember pedaling into a fierce headwind over the causeway, and my body groaning because the layoff had stiffened me up quite a bit. I recall passing motorists honking their horns to cheer me on and even a few passengers smiling and hanging out their windows. I can close my eyes and still see the flashing lights of the escorting police cars. I remember a lot about that day, but Ron's voice made that experience special.

Ron caught a bad hamstring cramp as we got back on our bikes and escorted me in the back of one of the police cars. With a massive smile on his face, Ron kept excitedly screaming, "One man can change the world. One man CAN change the world," over and over again as a mix of tears and sweat streamed down my face.

One man really can change the world.

Feeling is Seeing

Phoenix, Arizona. 2009

Of the many embraces I've had, one of the more extraordinary was a group hug in 2009.

In January of that year, an article I wrote for ESPN about my travels resonated with people globally. Almost overnight, thousands of emails from around the planet poured into my inbox. Most notes were short and sweet, saying 'thank you,' but others vividly described how my story helped them cope and move forward from their issues: abuse, mental illness, and other things. One person even wrote about their battle with addiction and said that my story helped them "stay clean for a day, thank you."

Reading people's accounts of how my quest for another hug helped them made me think deeper about my actions and explore my connection with people.

Even though I hadn't planned on bicycling North America again, I was inspired to make another trip and wanted to do more heartfelt than just pedal from coast to coast.

It took a little while to come up with an idea, but I eventually came up with the idea of bicycling across the country and using my off days of cycling to volunteer at a local charity.

Planning a bike trip across the USA is tough enough, but converting my journey into a one-man campaign of hugs, high5s, smiles, and service was exhausting.

Every day after work, I compared and contrasted different bike routes until I settled on one. Then, I approximated what cities I would be in each week and began making calls to organize my visits.

I called over fifty charitable organizations operating in cities along my route. My pitch was simple, "Hi, I'm Dave Sylvester, and I'm cycling across the United States this summer and would like to volunteer a day at your charity."

Not all of the responses I received were positive or kind, but that didn't matter. The details of the people's letters to me were etched on my mind and driving me in ways that nothing had before.

When people at some organizations laughed at me—yes, that did happen a few times—I would think, "You can laugh at me, but you can't stop me," and hang up to call someplace else.

It took months to finalize the tour details, and I was beyond proud of what I put together.

It took months to finalize the tour details, and I was beyond proud of what I put together. My cycling trip would begin on July 4, 2008, and I would volunteer at these charities:

> **San Diego, California:** Father Joe's Mission.
>
> **Phoenix, Arizona:** The Foundation for Blind Children.
>
> **Las Cruces, New Mexico:** Mesilla Valley Hospice.
>
> **El Paso, Texas:** Dismas Charities.
>
> **Austin, Texas:** The Lance Armstrong Foundation.
>
> **Galveston, Texas:** YMCA.
>
> **Galveston, Texas:** Wright Cuney Recreation Center.
>
> **New Orleans, Louisiana:** New Orleans SPCA
>
> **Mobile, Alabama:** Penelope House.
>
> **Nashville, Tennessee:** Campus for Human Development, a comprehensive homeless shelter.
>
> **Nashville, Tennessee:** Magdalene House.
>
> **Washington, DC:** Walter Reed Medical Center.

I scheduled my trip to end in New York City at the World Trade Center Memorial on September 11, 2008

With the itinerary laid out, getting press was next on the list, and then, it was off to San Diego to begin biking the nation!

My tour began smoothly with me volunteering at a San Diego homeless shelter and pedaling east toward Phoenix.

The day before bicycling into Phoenix, Ingrid Vanderveldt, an entrepreneurial event organizer, contacted me with an opportunity to deliver a 5-minute speech of my story to "warm-up" the crowd before the main speaker. Within 24 hours, I reached the venue, clueless about what I would say, but knew I would say it with a lot of enthusiasm.

I bounded onto the stage like a massive ball of positive energy, and the audience's response was warm, supportive, and immediate. The crowd encouraged me to go beyond my five-minute limit and shouted, "You are doing so much; what can we do for you?"

That question never entered my mind before speaking, and I blurted, "uhhhhh...I don't know; buy a tandem bicycle for the blind kids where I am volunteering tomorrow."

"Ok, I will," an audience member shouted.

"Me too," another voice shot out.

"Yeah, me too!" another person said.

Hearing this made me feel even more connected to the audience, and I stepped off the stage into a sea of hugs, high5s, and warmth.

Every charity visit on this tour was a first for me, so I had no idea what to expect when I walked through their doors. But, I can tell you that The Foundation for Blind Children in Phoenix was beyond impressive. More than just a building that housed an organization, The Foundation is a comprehensive campus and resource for anyone of any age in the nation suffering from vision impairment.

During my day, I met blind people of all ages who shared how The Foundation assisted them through every aspect of their life.

At the end of my day of service, I had the opportunity to address a small group of the Foundation's students. Excited to share the news of my gift, I glossed over my story and went right to the tandem bicycles. All of the students expressed their appreciation for my gift, but one seemed puzzled by it all. All of the students expressed their appreciation for my gift, but one seemed puzzled by it all.

"You aren't blind and have no connections to anyone in Phoenix or Arizona... this is cool and all, but I still don't get it: why?" he asked.

One of the administrators admonished him, calling his words "rude," but I thought they were valid and did my best to answer.

Seated in a room full of people who couldn't see me, I spoke in-depth about my friendship with Kevin and how deeply the emotional responses to my ESPN piece touched me. I also shared a story of how a blind Kenyan cyclist opened up my mind to the power of a smile.

The cyclist I spoke of was a Kenyan handicapped cycling team member and joined our group while we were biking in their country. This man would pedal along on the back of a tandem with a huge grin, no matter the conditions; uphill, downhill, windy, hazy, hot, or humid.

One particularly sweltering day, I was fixing a flat on the side of the road and looked up from my bike just as the tandem was biking past. As they passed me, I caught a glimpse of his smile that was so bright that it made me think, "What's he smiling about?"

The rest of the cycling day was pretty much all uphill through a humid haze, and I was miserable upon reaching camp. My mood only worsened when I saw that the only shady place to sit was in a small area by our support vehicle that was already crowded with every other dirty, dusty, stinky, and grumbling rider.

"This sucks," I thought.

To cool off, I grabbed some water from a giant metal communal water container, but a rider left it sitting in the sun. Once the hot water hit my lips, I snarled, "This day is fucked up!" to no one in particular. Every rider crammed in the shady area agreed with me except the blind Kenyan, who piped up and smilingly said, "It is a beautiful day!"

Wiping away some sweat from my eyes, I stared at his grin and thought, "Shit, he's still smiling??" His smile and genuine happiness eroded my embittered mood as it also reminded me that I take a lot for granted.

"I should smile more," I thought.

After relaying this story to the students at The Foundation, we began a lively conversation about what makes us smile. The emotion within the discussion of personal happiness prompted one of the kids to offer me a hug, which I gladly accepted. But, I was unprepared for the experience that occurred.

I know that blindness forces individuals to view inanimate objects with their hands and sense of touch, but never thought of that process when they viewed living things—how does it feel to be seen in that manner?

Well, let me tell you, it is absolutely electrifying.

As one student began hugging me, the others joined in. Each touch in this group embrace was different and unique, each touch, "seeing" me differently.

One touch was light and deft as it went over my back and shoulders. Another was firmer on my skin and firmer still at my joints. Another almost massaged my body.

Each press and knead saw deeper into me to the point that I found myself being viewed like never before. This hug was more than a random physical occurrence; it was a beautiful, emotional experience.

And I wasn't the only one who felt something, the student who questioned me wiped a tear and said, "I get you, man."

Hugged Out

West Texas. 2009

It isn't often that I get tired of hugging people, but I did in Balmorhea, Texas.

I was cycling across North America for a second time—San Diego, California to Philadelphia—and began my day in El Paso, Texas.

My plan was to begin cycling around 6:30 a.m. and go 80+ miles along US 10 to Sierra Blanca, Texas, and things started out perfectly. But by 8:30, everything changed.

The wind shifted against me, the temperature crept up by the minute, and humidity turned everything soupy. I biked slowly for about 50 miles and grabbed some lunch at a Fort Hancock truck stop, but nothing seemed to re-energize me. I sat at my table, sweating buckets and gave myself a pep talk to get through the rest of the day.

The next 30 miles were a struggle.

When I reached Sierra Blanca, I had no water, no snacks, and no strength to move forward. There was also another problem: the town was a lot smaller than I'd researched, and I couldn't find a hotel. I biked to a store, thinking that a bit of food and drink would pep me, but they were going out of business and had only Doritos and warm Dr. Pepper.

Shit.

Though I didn't want to, I began pedaling ahead and regretted my decision within a few miles. The best way to explain it was that my body blew up.

Every part of my body ached and sweated, and I was paying more attention to potential places I could rest than the road ahead of me. I was miserable and just stopped on the roadside in the blazing sun to get a break. I can't recall how long I was on the roadside, but I must've looked pretty pitiful because a family in a minivan pulled over to see if I needed help.

Initially, I refused any help. When the woman in the passenger seat produced an ice-cold bottle of water from an ice chest I changed my mind.

I changed my mind about everything.

The next thing I knew, my bike was broken down and stowed, and I had wedged myself in the middle of the backseat with their children. I wish that I could tell you more about the family—their kids, their ages, where they were from or going, or anything like that—but being nestled in the back seat gave me the full blast of the air conditioner and I passed out.

And I am not taking artistic license here: I truly passed out. How do I know?

I know this because they picked me up ten miles or so beyond Sierra Blanca, and when I woke up, we were well past the next town of Van Horn, Texas. For those unfamiliar with Texas, that means this family drove me 67 miles while I was sleeping. When I asked why they didn't just drop me off in Van Horn, they said that they did stop, but I was soundly sleeping and didn't want to wake me.

"Besides," the woman said with a smile, "...we love your story, and that town wasn't worthy of you."

The town that the family deemed "worthy" of me was Balmorhea, Texas, 189 miles from El Paso. The hotel where they dropped me off—and paid for my room—was a small independent one with a charming little restaurant attached. After hugging the family good-bye, I walked into the hotel with one agenda: get some food, drink, and plenty of rest.

I was so focused on eating and resting that I didn't even change and just walked into the restaurant wearing my bike gear. My clothes and food order of a pitcher of iced tea and two entrees before I even sat down drew every patron's attention.

Now usually, I welcome the opportunity to speak to people—but I was too worn out, and didn't want to be bothered. So, I grumpily answered when my waitress began questioning me about where I was going, and my past travels. I gave curt responses and was downright rude when the whole restaurant began to question me. I was so tired that I built a bit of a dark wall around me and plowed through my food.

Then an elderly woman seated at a table with three younger men (her sons, I assumed) pointed at me and asked, "So let me get this straight. You are just bicycling around the country, volunteering places, and hugging people?"

"Yup."

"For free?"

"Yup," I said, not even looking up, continuing to eat.

From that point on, no one said anything to me until the elderly woman began to stand up with the aid of her walker. The three men with her fell right into their roles: one watcheded over her as she stood up, another began shifting chairs to clear a path for her walker, and the third man paid the bill. Once standing, the tiny and frail woman waved them off and pointed in my direction.

Assuming that she was pointing toward the bathroom, I pretty much ignored this woman until she shuffled to my tableside and said something that cut right through all of my attitude. "Who hugs you—because you look like you could use one."

And then she bent down to hug me.

Angels in the Airfield

Mohawk, Tennessee. 2008

I met John Cooper outside a convenience store while waiting out the rain on my second bicycle trip across North America. The cashiers told him about my story, and he was so enamored by it that he walked right up to me and said, "Hey Big Fella, I hear you have quite the story."

His introduction began a short conversation about what I was doing, where I was going and led to an invitation for a tour of his airfield. "It's right on your way; you can't miss it," he said.

Always up for meeting new people, I obliged and pedaled my "Obama for President"-stickered bicycle up the road until I saw his "McCain for President"-stickered truck parked outside a small airplane hangar.

Just as I entered the hangar, heavy rain began to fall, and John happily greeted me with, "Looks like you're just in time."

The sound of the raindrops hitting the hangar provided the perfect background noise for further conversation about John's life, his love of flying, and my asking questions about some of his vintage aircraft. The more we spoke, the more John felt like an old friend.

John must have felt comfortable too because, after about 45 minutes, he said that he wanted to introduce me to his parents. With John being around 70, I thought his notion was odd, but went with it and said, "Okay, yeah, sure."

Taking a step from the hangar and into the rain, John shielded his eyes and quietly spoke. "Mom, Dad, I want you to meet a pretty cool fella..."

Initially, I didn't get up to see to whom he was talking, but the more he spoke, the more interested I became and stepped out from the hangar's cover.

Now standing with John and straining to see through the heavy rain, I followed his gaze toward a two-story farmhouse and assumed that his folks were resting beneath two nearby headstones. This tender parental introduction made me want to stay and talk with John all day, but I had to leave and get some miles before nightfall. As we hugged each other, he said, "Good luck out there."

As I was putting on my rain gear to leave, John said. "I was waitin' for the rain to stop...You've had a bike's-eye view of the world, and I wanted to take you up and be the one who gave you a bird's-eye view of things."

What an awesome dude.

Three days later, I was now in the southwestern corner of Virginia, still biking, and it was still raining. Nothing had changed much, and with a miserable forecast of unseasonably cold and heavy rain for a few days, nothing was going to change. I looked forward to getting on my bike and finding a nice steady pace to hold for a few hours.

When on a long stretch of road, a pickup truck pulled directly beside me. I pulled over to the shoulder as much as possible but couldn't move too far with the roadside washed out. I gave a side-glance to the truck and wondered why this guy wasn't moving on, especially with no traffic in either direction. Then, in an instant, so much happened.

A single burst of gunfire went up in the air.

A haunting cackle came from the truck.

The sound of screeching tires filled the air as the truck sped away up the road.

I stopped my bike but then began shaking. Trying to make out some details of the truck and where it went through wet and fogging glasses, I grabbed my phone. No service.

Frightened and angry, I biked for a few minutes and stopped to look at my phone. No service.

I tried to bike ahead again, but my pedals were too caked with mud to get it together. I kept wondering where the truck was. Eventually, I gathered myself to bike some more, and when I stopped, there was still no service.

Frustrated and scared, I walked my bike ahead until my phone had a weak signal. I nervously tried calling the police but kept looking around thinking, was the truck ahead of me? Or was the cackling driver on some surrounding high ground waiting to shoot me? Why was this happening?

I tried another call to a friend.

The call looked like it was connected, but I heard nothing, and barked out the details of where I was just in case they were listening.

The next town was seven miles away, and while pedaling towards it and hopefully a police station, I thought about how few details I knew about this incident. I didn't know if the driver was male/female, black/white, or old or young. Other than having a gun, I didn't know much and felt almost foolish in reporting the incident.

I felt this until the officer said, "calm down."

Unaware if the officer was patronizing me or not, all of the emotions surrounding this frightening occurrence took hold of me, and I began to vent. Glaring at the officer, who happened to be standing in front of a large county map and a small map of the world, I snapped, "I will not calm down! Turn around and look at those maps!! Pick any point... chances are I've been there, and nothing like what happened today has ever happened in any of those places, ONLY HERE!"

I kept talking, "You have a problem here. There is a shooter out here in your community, and they are going to get bored of shooting guns in the air one day, but they ain't getting another shot at my black ass; I'm out!"

I bicycled to my hotel realizing I had another matter on my plate.

The friend I'd called earlier apparently could hear me clear as a bell, and when I didn't respond to anything they said, got distressed and called my mother. By the time I spoke with her, my mother was anxious and had left a thousand messages.

Still heated from the day's events, I got on the phone with her and declared, "No one cares! Who was I kidding in thinking that I was doing anything of value to change the world. I've just wasted time, energy, and money!! I am officially out of the human philanthropy business."

My mother let me rant, but when I stated that I was abandoning my planned mission and grabbing a bus back to Philadelphia, her voice changed. "Relax," she said, adding "rethink this in the morning—you don't quit things."

"Whatever," I thought as I hung up the phone and began arranging for a shuttle to take me to a bus station.

After securing the shuttle, I shut my phone off and finally allowed myself to release all of my emotions and began crying. I was scared, angry, and felt very vulnerable. I didn't want to quit but felt I had no choice and went to bed, ready to walk away from it all.

But my world was righted when I checked my voicemail later that night.

An unfamiliar but friendly voice said, "Hey buddy, this is John Cooper, the guy with the airfield. I know that you are a man on a mission, doin' good things and with a schedule, but I also know that it's raining and gonna keep raining, so if you need me to pick you up and take you wherever so you can stay on schedule...well, I'll do it. Like I said, this is John Cooper, and I just wanna know that you're safe. Take care, buddy."

This straightforward phone call from a stranger who treated me as a friend helped me digest the events of the day and strengthened my resolve. His voicemail restored my faith.

The next morning I spoke with my mother, and before I began bicycling, I yelled, "I'm back in business, baby!"

Rest in Peace, John W Cooper.
May 22, 1942–February 14, 2011.
You are my angel.

Me, My Doctor,
& Now You

Cannon Falls, Minnesota. 2011

To celebrate my successful self-publishing of *Traveling at the Speed of Life*, I wanted to bike North America for the third time, but all I could afford was half the country.

So I biked from Minneapolis to Philadelphia.

That was really all I could afford.

I was so broke on this trip that I didn't even have a bicycle and borrowed a rental bike from a local bike shop.

"Give me a bike for a month, and I will bring it back with a great story," I proposed. Thank you, Breakaway Bikes of Philadelphia, for taking me up on that deal! The bike was great, but an issue with the rear rim gave me a lot of flat tires.

That is where this story begins: on my second day, with my fourth flat, and thoroughly annoyed by it all.

After the flat, I walked my bike to a nearby bus stop bench to sit down and change my tire. That's when a late 80s early 90s Buick rolled up on me. Inside was an elderly white-haired man, who leaned across the empty passenger seat to ask if I needed any help.

"No," I replied.

"Are you sure?" he asked again.

Rethinking my answer, I said, "I'm cool, but I guess you can talk to me while I change it."

"Okay," he said.

We began a conversation that dwelled on my life and global bicycle travels, and what I hoped to accomplish with this tour. After fifteen or twenty minutes of life chatter, I was pretty much done with the tire, and so was my friend in the Buick.

Nodding toward a sleeping child in a car seat in his car's back, he said, "I gotta go, Dave—gotta get my grand-baby back to her mother. Travel safe!" I thanked him for our time and waved goodbye, figuring that we would never see each other again.

Fate and my rear rim had other plans.

A mile or so down the road, I heard the distinct and dreaded hisssssssssssssssssss of another flat tire. But, unlike my last flat, there was no bench near.

This left me standing on the side of the road, trying to fix my flat quickly. As I did, the same Buick rolled up on me. Everything was just like it had been a few miles before, except this time, the old man got out of the car.

As he approached me, I could see that his eyes were puffy as if he'd been crying, and before I could say anything, he blurted out, "Hey man, glad I found you—listen, I don't have much time left." He paused to choke back a tear. "I got a bad diagnosis a little while ago, and I just don't—have—have much—time. I haven't told my family yet, and the only people that know this are me, my doctor, and NOW YOU," he said, pointing to the center of my chest.

With tears now streaming freely down his cheeks, he leaned back to sit on the hood of his car and cried a bit more. After a few moments, though, he composed himself and blew his nose. Through some sniffling, he shared that, since his diagnosis, he had been consumed with thoughts of "the world that is being left to my grandchildren."

"It scares me," he said.

He didn't say anything for a few moments, then added, "But speaking with you for a few minutes made me feel better about the world, and I just want to say: Thank You."

He said, "Thank you," again, emphatically pointed to, and touching my chest. He also declared that he would share everything with his family that afternoon. Stunned, I stood and cried with the man and then hugged him. He offered me a ride as he got back in his car, but I declined.

Before driving off, he leaned over to smile and yell, "Keep going, man!"

Ten Years Gone

Central Pennsylvania. 2011

When you are in the middle of nowhere and biking down a mountain, you don't expect to see much on the roadside. You may see a few dead animals, an errant truck tire, or some debris, but you certainly don't expect to see some random guy walking down the mountain.

But, that is precisely how I met Ryan McHenry, a guy running across the United States.

Without much of a road shoulder, I slowed down as soon as I approached Ryan to give us both space. As I slowed down, I looked at Ryan's gait and thought, "There's a guy without a care in the world."

"What's up?" I said as I slowly biked past him.

I stopped about 10–15 feet in front of him and then got off my bike to properly introduce myself and asked where he was going.

"I'm running across the United States," Ryan said, extending his hand to shake.

"No shit," I said.

"No shit," he replied.

Our "no shits" began a thoroughly engaging conversation that took us down the mountain, up another pass, into a town, and still talking as we entered a gas station convenience store to get something to eat.

By that time we were sitting atop a bent-up guardrail outside the gas station eating lunch, Ryan's friend Nick, who had been his support driver, had joined us. I was utterly enthralled with our chat and could've sat there for hours because speaking with Ryan was like talking to me during my first trip back in 2002.

Like me, Ryan began his journey across the United States after the untimely death of someone very close to him.

Like me, Ryan didn't care to speak much about the weather, gear, national landmarks, logistics, or anything related to his trip. All Ryan wanted to talk about was people he encountered were changing his feelings on many issues.

The same thing happened to me in 2002.

Back then, I remember feeling a significant loss about my friend Kevin's death, which prompted some vengeful emotions. But, after my bike trip across the nation, I cared more about the opportunities within life and living than anything that surrounded death.

Opening up about his life, Ryan said, "I am not angry anymore. Upset, yeah— but not, not—angry." He followed up with, "Is that real? Did that happen to you?"

All I could do was smile and say, "Yeah."

Our talk continued until late afternoon, and then it was time for us to go to our hotels. When I hugged Ryan and Nick goodbye, I didn't think that I would see them again, but fate had other plans.

A massive rainstorm settled into the valley the next morning, and as I sat in a diner waiting for it to pass, who should walk by but Ryan and Nick. Our faces lit up upon seeing each other, and as we embraced, Ryan said, "It was meant to be, brother."

The three of us sat in a corner booth and talked about our possible futures for an hour or so until the rain died down and it was time for us to begin the last legs toward our final destinations. I hugged Ryan one last time and told him that his future was bright.

He said, "After talking to you, I think so, too."

Ryan and I have remained in touch, and he is now a doctor, father, and an even more chill and awesome dude living in Southern California.

I Wanted To Stop

Richland Center, Wisconsin. 2011

Meet Leroy.

We met in Richland Center, Wisconsin, on my third bicycle trip across the United States. I was grabbing lunch at an American Legion bar and chatting with the bartender, who cut me off and said, "Leroy's coming here soon, and he's gonna love you!."

With this being my first visit to Richland Center, I was clueless about knowing a man named Leroy or anyone else in this community, but the bartender was right. Leroy loved me.

Even though we never met, I knew who Leroy was as soon as he entered the bar. Greeted enthusiastically, like he was on the TV show, "Cheers" with a big "Hey Leroy!"—it was obvious. An old black man with a warm smile, Leroy's face lit up upon hearing his name. He waved to the bar and then made his way around the room, like he owned the place, exchanging pleasantries and jokes with almost every patron.

In watching Leroy 'work the room', one could feel his charm. He was so smooth about things that you almost didn't notice that he hobbled a bit and had a cane. As he spoke to people, it was apparent from the glances that came my way that Leroy was also getting bits and pieces of my story.

After about 15 minutes of this, Leroy walked over to the barstool next to me, placed his hand on my shoulder, and said, "Man, you are a big dude. Now, let me hear your story in YOUR words."

After hearing my story, Leroy shared that he motorcycled across the nation shortly after WWII with some of his war buddies. Hearing this prompted me to ask why.

"To see what I fought for," he said plainly and adding, "...But, I really wanted to do what you are doing."

With great excitement, I said, "You wanted to ride a bike!"

"Fuuuuuuuuuuck no! And the more that I think about you biking around, the crazier I think you are. You see that I am sitting on this side of you, facing away from the window. I don't even want to see your bike outside!"

"No, man. I wanted to stop. I wanted to stop and see things, stop, and ask questions. I just wanted to stop and be."

Leroy wanted to stop in different places, couldn't in some places, shouldn't in other places, and didn't in most places. "We didn't dare—it was a different America then." Leroy's voice trailed off for a bit as he scanned the room.

Then, he turned to me and asked, "How do you stop? I mean, I don't even know if I would have stopped in this place—and I KNOW these people."

I told him that I believed that I could read people well.

He said, "You must," looking around the room with a smirk.

I also said that anyone, even the most racist person in the world, could put up with someone long enough to put a couple of dollars for a sandwich and a Gatorade in their pocket.

A lone white man seated at the bar raised his glass and said, "Cheers to that." Not knowing if the patron was toasting to being a racist or not, Leroy just looked at me and said, "SEE, I have no idea what he is toasting to—the fact that you read people well, or that he hates black folks."

We laughed for a bit, and when I asked for more details of his life, like his age, he gave me a riddle. "I worked for 32 years, retired for 32 years, was in WWII, and have seen a lot—you figure it out."

Rolling my eyes, trying to figure it out, I stopped myself and said, "Ahh, it doesn't matter."

"Nope, it doesn't," he said.

As I gathered my stuff to leave, he scribbled his number down on some scrap paper and said to call him if I got into any trouble. He cautioned me, though, that I might have to wait a bit for him to get there if I did. Holding up his cane, he said, "I don't move like I used to, brother. But, know that once I get there, IT'S ON!"

It has always been my ability to move forward that has earned respect, praise, and comments—never my stopping.

In all honesty, it is when I have had to stop on my journeys to hitch a ride when I was sick on the road, and at other times that have brought me a lot of personal anguish that caused me to view myself as weak.

Leroy put everything in a whole new light and showed me that my stopping made all of the difference.

The Only Motherfucker

Even though we all know that it is never good news when the phone rings at 3:00 a.m., we answer it anyway. I am no different.

I groggily answered the phone with a gruff "hello" and heard a man's voice ask, "Is this Dave Sylvester?" Fearing that someone I knew was in some trouble, I immediately sat up straight and said, "Yeah."

"You probably don't remember me, but we met a while ago, and I was thinking of killing myself when I was making your breakfast," was how he launched into the conversation.

Riveted by his opening statement, and from the fact it was apparent this man was crying, I listened to him intently and soon realized that I did recall meeting him.

I cut him off and said, "Ohhhhhhh yeah, man, I remember you."

"You do?"

"Yeah," I said. "We chatted during breakfast."

"No," he snapped, "that isn't what happened."

He told me that I'd been the only customer in the cafe that morning and asked

109

if I could talk to him while he made my breakfast. He said that because of his depressed mood and bitterness, he didn't want to speak to anyone and asked me, "Why?"

He said that was when I looked around the cafe and said, "Because you're the only motherfucker here."

Yeah, that sounds like me, I thought, and said, "Oh yeah."

"That was the first laugh I had since being discharged from the military," he said and added that listening to my life stories really lifted his mood.

"I felt so good; I gave you some extra food," he said.

Now THAT is what my greedy ass remembered.

"You remember what happened next?"

"Yeah, I ate my food."

"NO," he snapped again.

Well, shit, why don't you tell me what happened? I thought.

As if on cue, he told me that after placing my food in front of me, he asked if he could sit with me while I ate, and I asked, "Why?"

"Because you're the only motherfucker here," he'd said.

"And you know what? I laughed—again! That was a test for me. That second laugh meant that the first laugh was REAL!"

He said that he'd laughed all day about our exchange.

Amused by his story, but still somewhat unclear as to why he was calling, I asked, "Soooooooooooo, what's up, man?"

"Don't you get it? Dude—you are saving lives." What? I thought.

Again, almost on cue, he repeated, "You are SAVING lives!!"

I didn't know what, if anything, to say. So I sat silent and listened. He shared that he was in bad shape, just like when we first met.

"But," he added, "it just occurred to me that maybe I'm not so fucked up because I'm not doing what I normally do—in these times. I am crying, but I'm laughing too because I am thinking of you—thank you."

His call of gratitude was a very emotional one to receive, and by the time we hung up, I had made myself a cup of tea and was thinking about the other people I had encountered on my travels.

The thought of "saving people's lives" was kind of intense, and I needed a bit of levity—so when he thanked me for picking up the phone and talking, I couldn't help but say, "No sweat, man. I'm the only motherfucker here."

The Enchanted Mind

Kingsessing Avenue.

We all grow up idolizing someone: stronger, more athletic, more intelligent, more handsome, more pretty, or more something...than us.

These idols are smart when you are childish, witty when you are crass, and smooth when you are perpetually awkward.

You know the feeling.

They seem to do everything right, while you do everything wrong—and because of that, you grow up looking at them with a sort of glow and enchanted reverence.

My idol was a pair of twins, Kevin and Kelvin Bowser, and all that meant was that there were twice as many ways that I could pale myself in comparison to them.

In many ways they were the same: athletic, healthy, intelligent, opinionated, handsome, and genuinely likable.

In other ways they were different. One was always willing to rebel and fight from the outside-in while the other battled from the inside-out.

One was a meat-eater; the other was vegan. One was open to talking; the other, not so much. They were both good men.

As I grew, I became health-conscious, more intelligent, developed my own opinions, and became handsome, depending on how much one had to drink. (I should note that if one has a lot to drink, I become downright gorgeous!)

As I grew into my own, logic and reality took over. I knew that the only reason that I saw the Bowser Twins in this idolizing and enchanting way was that they were older. But even though I knew they were just as human as I was, all they had to do was occupy a room that I was in, and it all came flooding back.

I would become a kid again, watching them with an idolizing eye and thinking of them with an enchanted mind. A lot of time has passed since I was a kid, and the passage of time has brought a lot of change.

Kevin, a 9/11 casualty is gone.

Kelvin has been stricken with a neurological issue that has left him to labor with crutches and halting speech.

And me—a drunk driver hit me a few years ago, and now I'm limping more often than not.

I also don't have the free time that I used to, so I don't see Kelvin much. But when we do, it is hard for me to see past the crutches and hear beyond the impaired speech.

Sadly, time has robbed me of my enchantment.

But when I entered a crowded restaurant one Saturday night to honor Kelvin for his 31 years of service as an IRS agent, it returned.

The re-enchantment didn't happen as soon as I entered the room and hugged Kelvin, but it took hold moments later when I said that I would try to find my seat. That was when, out of all the seats in the restaurant, Kelvin patted the chair next to his and said, "You're right here."

I didn't notice everything at first, but as I sat next to Kelvin and watched him stand to accept congratulating hugs, I heard his familiar laugh and felt Kevin's presence as his name was also mentioned more and more; I felt that old enchantment return and it was like I was a kid again.

Nah, it was better than those days, because I was now cool too.

I left as the night neared an end—no goodbyes, no farewell hugs. Yeah, it was rude, but I didn't want to break the spell by officially saying, "goodbye."

I just wanted to see Kelvin as I had when I was a kid and feel like Kevin was very much alive, but just in another room, if only for a moment—if only in my enchanted mind.

Saying The Wrong Thing
—In The Worst Way—
At The Right Time

Boston, Massachusetts. 2015

After lecturing at Northeastern University, I killed time in a South Station cafe waiting for my train back home to Philadelphia.

Without any work to do, I partook in my favorite activity, people-watching, and noted five or so guys seated near me who seemed to be doing the same thing.

One of the guys loudly cracked a joke that got all of us laughing, and I used that as an opening to introduce myself and ask the guys what they were meeting about.

To a man, they each tersely said, "nothing" and then quickly asked me what I was doing in Boston. I explained that I had been lecturing and went into my backstory.

When most people hear my story, they want to listen to specifics about where I have been and other details—hottest, coldest, friendliest, and so on—but not this group.

Nope, after only a few superficial questions, this group wanted only to speak of the tougher times that I encountered while traveling. Many of their questions wanted to drill down on my thought process at the beginning of my story when I lost my friend Kevin.

"How did you find it within you to move forward and not stall out?"

Before I go on, let me tell you that I curse a lot. It bothers my family and some of my old teachers, but it is what I do. After laughing and joking with this group of guys, I felt the freedom to say whatever I wanted, however I wanted.

"Life will fuck you," I said, "because that's what it does."

"I believe that it (life) throws things at you that you didn't want or think you can deal with, but you can. I don't always like it, but I believe that's what life does, so that's what I deal with. AFTER life fucks you, though, it is up to you to deal with it and move forward, not relive it in your head repeatedly and whine about shit, because that isn't livin' to me. Life has and will fuck me, but after that, I do all I can to move forward. Because then, I DO ALL THE FUCKIN'! And I like to fuck!"

Feeling that I was on a roll, I recounted a bunch of times I had something terrible happen in my life and then use it as motivation: Kevin dying on 9/11 led to my biking the US; getting hit by a car and working my ass off to limp, but be able to bicycle Asia; I didn't get a publishing deal, but did all that I could to research things and become a successful self-published author.

I could have listed a few more examples, but it was close to my train's departure, so I ended with, "After life fucked me, I did all the fuckin'." Right before I left, I emphatically high5'd each man as I said each word of, "I—do—all—the—fuckin'. Now y'all go out and do the fuckin'. I gotta train to catch."

When I give talks, I "read the room" to evaluate what I believe I can get away with and felt I had read this room correctly. As I assessed it, this was a "drop the mic" moment for me.

But the response I received belied that.

These guys said nothing; I mean, absolutely nothing. There was nothing but an awkward period of silence like I farted or something. It was so awkward that I didn't even hand them a copy of my book. I just tossed it to one of the guys and backed out of the cafe.

Two months later, I got a thank you email from one of the guys that also explained their silence. I had stumbled upon a support group for men who had been sexually assaulted—and I had given them a new way of looking at things to move forward and their meetings had taken an entirely different bend since meeting me.

"Keep being you—you're one of a kind," the man wrote.

Once You Create Art: It Ain't Yours

Not many things stop me from talking, but during the Q&A at a university lecture, one student completely shut me up.

Seated at the head of an amphitheater classroom next to the professor, I fielded questions ranging from what it was like to write *Traveling at the Speed of Life* to my thoughts on the various countries I traveled through.

Almost 30 minutes into the session, one female student in the back row raised her hand.

"Yes," I said.

The student then lowered her hand, took a deep breath, paused for a moment, and pronounced, "I just want to say thank you for writing this book. I was raped and—naming one particular chapter—really helped me deal with it, and I'm gonna be like you and repurpose my emotions into something good to help people."

The student's statement would have been highly impactful if she said this one-on-one, but her words' honoring effect was only magnified by us being in a crowded classroom. The already silent room somehow became even quieter. I said nothing for a few moments and then, without moving my lips, whispered, "What do I say to that?" in the professor's direction.

But, the professor wasn't there. She had somehow quietly eased her chair away from me and was now practically sitting with the students and whispered, "It's your show."

A few more moments went by, and I looked up at the woman and said, "I don't know what to say."

"There really is nothing to say just: Thank You," she replied.

"Thanks," I said, and then after yet another pause, I inquired, "Not for nothing, but check it: what was the passage that helped you?" The student then grabbed her dog-eared copy of my book and opened it up to the select page. As she read the passage that moved her, I recalled writing it and smirked a bit.

"What's so funny?" she asked.

"Nothing at all," I said as I looked at my words on the page and added, "it's just that I remember writing that, and I was setting you (the reader) up for the money-shot two paragraphs down the page."

Upon saying that, the only sound heard in the classroom was the rustling of pages as the students grabbed their copies followed by silence while they read what I believed to be the evocative blurb.

Moments later, the student smiled as she cleared her throat and said, "Nah, that didn't do a damn thing for me."

Like I said, once you create art, it ain't yours.

Up, Up and Away In
My Beautiful Balloon

Scituate, Massachusetts.

April 19, 2013, was the first time I heard the term: Shelter in Place.

I was on my way to a book signing in Scituate, Massachusetts and the nation was still reeling from the Boston Marathon bombing four days before. The night before heading up, a shootout with the perpetrators occurred in Boston and they were still at large, so I took the bus—thinking it could detour more quickly if need be.

The entire trip was weird from the very beginning. There were only four passengers on the bus for starters, and all we did was speak about what was going on in Boston. "It is a six hour journey from Philadelphia to Boston and while there was a flurry of updates for the beginning of the journey, there wasn't much news for the last couple of hours. I thought that things had calmed down but, as we approached the exit for Boston's South Station, the bus was waved down by a State policeman in full riot gear.

All of the passengers went to the front of the bus as the driver opened the door.

"What're you doing," the cop said.

"Drivin' a bus," the driver said, dripping with sarcasm that would've made me laugh any other time.

"Well...Boston is closed."

"What??" the driver said.

Wait, let me be honest. I don't know if the driver really said what?? But I know that I said it—along with the other riders.

125

"Boston is under a shelter in place order. Drop 'em off around the corner."

Still unaware of what 'shelter in place' meant exactly, I got the gist immediately when I saw the deserted streets and a strong police presence everywhere.

When I reached my friend's place in Scituate, the only conversation topic was the continued manhunt for the remaining bomber that had progressed into a door-to-door search in a Watertown neighborhood. Then, there was a news-break; the remaining bomber was in a stand-off with the police.

We ran from the dining room to then huddle around the TV in the living room. As we looked for updates, we also kept asking one of the dinner guests, who was the mother of a SWAT sergeant, what was going on.

We continued looking back and forth from the TV to the woman reading her son's texts forever, it seemed but then there was a break.

"THEY GOT 'EM!!" the woman screamed.

And, then 30 seconds later, the news channels announced, "They got him!!"

With those words, I could feel the state of Massachusetts erupt with cele-bration. Within moments, people poured out of their homes to party in the streets. It was like a New Year's Day in April.

Everyone drank way too much that night, including myself, and I woke up thinking, "This whole state is gonna be suffering from the same hangover I have. No one is gonna show up to my book signing. It's gonna be a complete failure."

Just the thought of having a book signing with no one attending hurt, and I went for a walk to sulk. About 20 minutes into my walk, I got a text from a random number that said: I love this fuckin' book!! Thank you for writing it!

With those words was a picture of someone in Texas who took my book up in a hot air balloon. I stopped in the middle of the street and thought, "Everything's gonna be alright,"

And it was. The book signing was packed, and I sold out of books.

Thank you, Angie.

Dapper Dan

Austin, Texas. 2013

With a few hours to kill between giving lectures at St Edward's University, I elected to go by a nearby animal shelter to pet/hug some dogs.

Practically all of the dogs at the shelter were eager to play. But, one dog cowered at the back corner of his cage as I even looked his way.

I asked one of the shelter workers what was wrong with the dog, and they said that "Dapper" had been severely abused and starved. "Dapper needs all the love he can get," they said.

Because of his previous conditions, Dapper was afraid of everything and was especially fearful of me as I attempted to pet him. A mix of maybe a pit-bull and a boxer, something about Dapper drew me in and made me want to do something to connect with him. With his cage door fully opened, Dapper cowered even deeper into the corner and ignored me even as I put some treats on my hand.

"You're just too big, Dude," a shelter worker said.

Refusing to let my size stop something good from happening, I put some treats in my hand and then laid on the floor to make myself 'smaller' than Dapper and I waited. Though it took a while, Dapper eventually—and literally—inched over to me and cautiously ate the treats out of my hand. I never actually was able to pet Dapper, only scratch a few whiskers on his chin, but it felt great.

After a few minutes of this, I slowly got up on all fours and got 'bigger,' and Dapper backed away. He didn't totally retreat into his cage, though, which we all took as a good sign.

Most people around the planet know me as "Big Dave" and for my hugs but there's a rescue pup in Texas named Dapper that recognizes me as "Small Dave" and for a few chin scratches.

That's cool with me.

Tony Montana Was Right

Sydney, Australia, 2014

Before bicycling Australia, my friend Brigette, who works at the University of Technology in Sydney, arranged for me to speak to a group of Aboriginal students taking part in a summer youth program at the university. Their visit to Sydney was a first for seeing any metropolis, and most of the students took a two-day train ride to reach the city.

Introducing the students to the world through my embracing pictures and stories was an honoring experience. They loved my talk, but one student in attendance looked past my hugs and really connected with my high5s.

After my talk, a big, personable teen with an equally big smile approached me while boarding a bus to take a tour of Sydney. He said that he felt my boldness in asking random strangers for high5s was "fearless."

"I've never seen anything like this. But," he practically whispered, "what if they say no?"

"To what?"

"The high5s."

"Then, they're missing out."

"On what?" he asked with an innocent curiosity.

"The magic," I said with a smile and a winking attempt—though I am horrible at winking.

Looking at me as if he were balancing out whether I was crazy or cool, the teen seemed intrigued. Once off the bus and standing on a busy Sydney street, the teen asked how many people I could high5 in ten minutes.

"I don't know. Start counting," I said and began to walk down the street, asking the world, "Who wants a high5?"

He would shout the number with every smack: "One—two—three," getting more and more excited with each one.

"Ten, eleven, twelve—" His voice grew louder. When I reached 17, he said, "Oh my God, he's going to get twenty," with zeal.

Just then, the 18th person declined. The kid was crestfallen, and so was I, to a certain extent—I really like high5s.

As the person walked away, the teen shouted, "Why would you walk away from a high5? Why would you walk away from this man? He came all the way from the States to bike here—he wrote a book. I haven't read it yet, but if this book is like him, then I know it's good." As is with teenagers, each of his sentences was more exciting than the previous one.

I said, "Relax. Dude, it's like I said: THEY are missing out, not me."

As also with teenagers, they're resilient. He quickly changed gears from the man walking away to looking at me and raising his hand to heartily high5 me.

"That's eighteen," he yelled. Adding, "You can still make twenty!"

After engaging the 19th person, I tried coaxing him into high5-ing the 20th person with me, but he shook his head, extended his arms, and said, "Noooo, no, that's you!! That's your world."

"No, the world is yours," I said.

As if being introduced to a new concept, the kid repeated the sentence a few times: "The world is yours."

He kept repeating it until I stopped him and said, "No, you don't say, 'The world is yours.' You say, 'The world is mine.'"

He again repeated the sentence, "The world is mine," with each utterance containing more emotion, depth and passion.

"The world is mine. **The world is mine**!!"

With each repetition of the phrase, "The world is mine", his smile grew broader, and I became more aware that the concept I freely embrace might take hold in him. He did eventually start high5-ing people with me and then went down a street by himself to do it on his own.

I do believe that one day we will read about this kid doing his own Hugs and High5s Tour.

Go High5 'em brother; THE WORLD IS YOURS!!

Keep Going

Gundagai, Australia 2014

My sciatic nerve gave me serious issues midway between Sydney and Melbourne on my Australian Hugs and High5s Tour.

The nerve's throbbing rendered my night sleepless and unable to cycle for more than a few miles. Within days, I couldn't bike and had to walk my bicycle down the Hume Highway. Exhausted, I openly wondered if I could make it through the day, let alone the rest of my trip.

I needed a break badly and entered a farm and feed store to get a rest. While resting, my nerve pain dissipated, and I chatted up the store clerk.

At one point, I leaned back on a very modern bookcase that seemed out of place in the store's utilitarian design. Examining the bookcase, filled with works by Mandela, Dale Carnegie, and Deepak Chopra, I asked why it was there.

The clerk said a town resident recently published a book about an American athlete and bought the case to encourage reading in the community.

Thinking aloud, I said it would be nice to speak with the author since I was recently published. Before I could say 'give her my email,' he was on the phone with who I assumed was her husband.

"Hey, yeah...there's a big American here that want to talk to your wife......
yeah....he wrote a book too...he just wants to talk...yeah..yeah, he's riding a
bike across Australia..well, to Melbourne.......someone died or something...
he just wants to talk......sure....yeah...sure.. look...look, I'll just send him
down. Okay....okay..yeah right now..okay bye."

He shushed me as I reached for the phone, saying afterward, "Okay, it's taken
care of. They live right down the road about half a kilometer on the right, next
to an old train shed. Finish up, they're expecting you."

"Thank you??" I thought.

I wasn't going to stop, but the clerk's directions were so precise, I thought,
"why not?"

There was one problem, though; the house was 30–40 yards beyond a DO NOT
ENTER gate. Looking past the sign at a mid-sized ranch house, I thought, "This
is how someone gets gruesomely killed in EVERY horror movie...No sane
person should walk that path."

...So, I unlatched the gate and took one bold step after another.

Suddenly, six barking dogs ran out from both sides of the house and quickly
surrounded me. I immediately stopped. The dogs calmed a bit—except for
one old dog who promptly lost interest and laid down.

Feeling that the dogs were more noisemakers than aggressors, I stayed still and
yelled, "Hey, anyone home??...It's the American writer from the store."

A thin woman wearing jeans, t-shirt, cowboy hat, and a puzzled expression
emerged from the house, hollering, "This is so random!"

I hollered back, 'It may be random, but that doesn't mean that it can't be
good."

It was the author, Rochelle Llewelyn Nicholls.

We approached each other to shake hands, and our collective smiles quickly
eased our apprehensions.

She invited me into her home for tea and joined by her husband Andrew, we
discussed everything from her attending college in Alabama to her husband

being a firefighter and more. But, with her soon to be released book *Joe Quinn Among the Rowdies*, she was eager to hear my thoughts on book promotions.

Meanwhile, the dogs that had scared me were now snuggling on their dog beds. But, sadly, it was time to leave.

She suggested I stop by The Niagara Diner in the next town as she wished me well. "They'll love you," she said.

Gundagai was the next town, and before visiting the diner, I checked into my hotel. As I filled out my registration card, the short, old, white-haired lady working the desk asked about my bicycle, mission, and other questions like; where was my support vehicle.

"I'm alone," I said.

Looking with disbelief and motioning with her thumbs as if texting, she asked, "Where're your...?"

"No social media people; I'm alone."

She rolled her eyes and waved me off as she marched right past me out the door to the street's edge. Turning to the left and right and seeing no vehicles or movement, she walked back to the door's threshold and flatly said, "No shit."

Keeping her unblinking eyes directly on mine, she reached into the register to grab the money that I just gave her for my room. Counting it out but withholding a 20, she placed the remainder on the counter and said, "Hey, I have to charge you something. "

After that, I decided to check out The Niagara Diner. Designed in art deco style, comfy booths, and pictures of Niagara Falls, NY, the diner reminded me of America. With only the diner staff around, I loudly asked for the best thing on the menu.

"Everything's great, but our fried chicken's the best," a guy wiping down the counter proclaimed.

"Well, fry it up," I said.

"Sure thing..where are you from?" the counter guy asked.

The counter guy's name was Tony, and he owned the cafe. We talked and discovered our shared love of chicken thighs, movies, and more throughout two orders of chicken. But where we connected was with our love of working out. While taking my last bites, Tony asked if I wanted to see his home gym, and when I said yes, he said, "Well, hurry up!"

Better equipped than some professional gyms I've seen, Tony's home gym in the cafe's basement immediately motivated me to ask, "Can I do a few reps of something?"

Pushing through sciatic pain, we did a chest workout, and by the time we walked upstairs to the diner, Tony was introducing me to cafe patrons as his "good friend." But, nightfall was approaching, and though I didn't want to, I had to leave.

Before entering my hotel room, I noticed that my lights were now on.

But I calmed down when I saw a pot of tea and a note waiting for me. The note from the front desk lady that just said: KEEP GOING.

It's A Small World After All

Melbourne, Australia. 2015

I've often heard that it's a small world, but I saw it firsthand when I visited a Melbourne, Australia "Tex-Mex" restaurant.

As soon as I walked in the eatery with my friend Cherie, my first move was to ask the waitress if they had good guacamole.

"Of course," she answered.

"Are you sure?" I asked, doubling down.

She emphatically assured me that they did, and doubled down by winking and stating: "I should know, I'm from Texas!" Our exchange spurred a conversation about what brought her to Oz from Texas and her years of partying since.

"But that's all behind me, now," she said.

She told me she'd gotten her life "back on track" by winning acceptance to a graduate program in Colorado, and was leaving Australia to go back home to the US in a few days.

"Yup, I'm wearing my big-girl panties," she said, "Sold all my stuff. Got rid of my car, and you are not only my last table of the night—you are my last table EVER!"

Her energizing story was totally unexpected and prompted me to reach inside my backpack to offer her a copy of my book. She asked what my book was about, and after explaining, she loudly exclaimed, "Holy shit! You hug people, right?? YOU'RE the reason my best friend and her mother biked across the United States last summer."

"W-what?"

The waitress explained that her best friend's mother attended the lecture of a "big black guy" in California and walked away inspired by his story, energy, and hugs. Her friend's mother was so inspired that she bicycled from San Diego to Florida the next year, with her daughter driving the support car.

"That's all you!" she exclaimed, "Holy shit!!"

The randomness of it all was unfathomable. As the waitress walked away to get our guacamole, I told my friend Cherie that I was so glad she was with me because "no one will believe this."

It happened to me, and I still find it unbelievable.

It truly is a small world, so be nice to people...you never know when you will meet them again.

G-Rated

Sydney, Australia. 2015

Sometime around 1:00 AM on January 1, 2015, I wandered into a Sydney, Australia bar in the Bondi Beach area feeling incredible.

My emotional glow was because I had just completed a Hug and High5 Tour of Australia.

This "tour" was a big step because it was my first solo international bike tour. Also—by bicycling from Sydney to Melbourne volunteering and hugging 1,000 random people in a month—this was the first tour that encapsulated my personal mission to positively engage people and help make them smile.

It wasn't easy. With no signage, no preamble, no advance team, or anything else really, the tour was mainly me encountering random people on my bike and asking, "Do you want a hug?"

But somehow, with that little plan in place, I was able to pull off my lofty goal of embracing 1,000 people in just 25 days!

So while everyone around me was in a drunken revelry over the dawn of a new year, I was more reflective. I sat at the bar, thinking about all the ideating, planning, saving, and work it had taken to make this tour a success. I struck up a conversation with some people seated around me, and one woman proclaimed, "You're the most positive man on the planet."

Considering the mood that I was in, it was a reaffirming statement, and doubly so when she snatched a coaster from behind the bar and told me to write something inspirational.

"Write now, right now," she yelled over the bar's music.

Feeling buzzed and not boozed just yet, I grabbed a pen and scribbled one of my G-rated mantras down. (I have a ton of R- and X-rated ones, trust me.)

"This is awesome," she said as she read it and hugged me.

More than 18 months later, I received an email from that woman with a picture of the coaster and a note saying that she'd recently moved and that my coaster was one of the few and "truest" things she had taken from her old place.

That said, here is what I wrote:

IMAGINE IT.
WORK IT.
BECOME IT!

Now go imagine, work and become.

A Moment Ago

2014

This book is a collection of hug essays and other random uplifting and provocative encounters I have had in my life since 2001. Many of these stories happened in one day, but other accounts took years to develop like this one.

I wrote this speech for my friend Michelle's sister, Sharon, whom I met shortly after my return from Africa in 2006, and who died in 2014.

Because she lived outside the city, Sharon and I only saw each other on occasions—holidays, BBQs, etc. But in the handful of times we met, what stood out about Sharon was her care and concern for her sister.

Whenever I saw her, Sharon always expressed her appreciation of the support I gave her sister Michelle, when Michelle's husband, Tom, was battling cancer. Because Sharon and I had only a few actual meetings, it was both surprising and an honor that her family selected me to be one of the speakers at Sharon's memorial. So before you read this, I guess what I am saying is that you don't have to see someone a lot to impact them.

♥ ♥ ♥

When Michelle first told me of Sharon's passing, I thought, "Oh my God, that can't be right—I just saw her a moment ago."

But then I thought, "No...I didn't. It wasn't a moment...it was more like a while ago."

Saddened and stunned, I walked away from Michelle, thinking about what moments mean.

More than just some well-defined piece of time—like a second, or a minute, or a beat—moments are unique unto themselves. Within them, are these dynamically mighty morsels of time, space, opportunity, and perspective.

Moments are those places in a story where we all just know to hold our collective breath.

What we say "in the heat of the moment" can start a vicious fight that can only be quieted by a tender "moment of forgiveness."

The friend that you treasure the most is one that you can depend on to be there—"on a moment's notice."

We instinctively hold ourselves to the person who looks us in the eyes and pleasantly and politely says, "One moment, please."

And we always envy the person who has a life where there's "never a dull moment."

Moments are something else, and *people* can be moments as well.

Surely you've encountered someone who entered a room and infused the atmosphere with more life, wisdom, and happiness than you thought the room could hold.

You felt it...the moment they walked in. Maybe you didn't notice their nuances while present, but I bet you took note of their light when everything felt dimmer...the moment they left.

Moments are tremendous but extremely difficult to recognize in real-time because moments need the courageousness of one to act upon it—right then, right there—otherwise, their immense potential is dormant.

I will be sincere: Sharon and I didn't interact that much, but I know she knew the power within a moment.

I know this because every time we met, she took me aside and thanked me for whatever comfort she felt I was giving her sister Michelle, and the rest of her family.

"You are and do good, David," she once told me.

Sharon didn't know that fate would have me speaking up here on her behalf on this day, but she knew to speak up.

She knew that we often let the moments of our lives slip by thinking that we will have more time, have another shot, or come across a better occasion to celebrate it all.

Sharon was brave enough not to let our moment slip by.

Someone has to be bold enough to step forward and say, "I love you"—to make that special "I love you too" moment happen.

Someone has to be fearless enough to seek out someone who isn't in a good mood just to hug them because they know that once they both feel the warmth and tenderness within that embrace—the spirit of the moment will be uplifted.

One person has to be mindful enough to step from their own circumstance to recognize and acknowledge another's best efforts and say, "I believe in you."

They do this knowing that if nothing is said, there's no possibility of a "bonding moment" later on when that person triumphs and genuinely says, "Thanks, I couldn't have made it here without you."

A step toward "a moment" is imperative. Otherwise, the vibrancy of the opportunity is lost and may be gone forever.

So while we are here to celebrate the beautiful moment that was Sharon's precious life—let's be like her and make a moment, a special moment right here, right now.

Let's do more than just look around at each other and think, "Man, I have really got to stay in touch with this one," or, "It's been too long since seeing that one."

Let's do more and take just—one—more—step—literally, to walk out and away from our comfort zones and go over to someone and say something:

Say: I love you.

Say: I believe in you.

Say: I am sorry.

Say: I promise to do better.

Say: Thank you—I admire you—I will stay in touch.

Say something funny, like, "I always thought you were cooler than me when we were kids."

Or say to someone like Sharon simply said to me, say, "You are good, and you do good."

Say whatever—it doesn't matter, but say something to someone and make this moment—real.

Do this now—because without recognizing, acknowledging and moving upon this amazingly brilliant morsel of opportunity we have before us, we all run the risk of someone in the future learning the circumstances of our fate and having them walk away thinking, "Oh my God, that can't be right...I just saw them...a moment ago.

The Ministry of Hugs

Orlando, Florida. 2016

After the Pulse Nightclub massacre, I went down to Orlando for a few days to offer what support and hugs I could to the community. Initially, I was nervous about how my actions would be perceived, but I soon calmed down because everyone took note of my actions' genuineness. But it seemed that as I walked around the growing tribute of flowers, balloons, pictures, and poems, people noticed other things.

A few hours before my flight home, an older man and woman from the Billy Graham Ministries approached me while sitting with some people.

Standing over me wearing matching khakis, polos, and lanyards with ID badges, they looked official and made me feel nervous. And when they said, "Hey, we've been watching you, big fella, and we want to talk to you," I felt even more nervous.

I excused myself from the people I was speaking with, and before I could even say much, one of them said, "We've been talking to some of the people you've hugged."

"Oh shit, what'd I do," I thought.

They said that they had approached some people I had spent time with, and "they all said the same thing; you're a cool dude, and that we should get a hug too."

Still thinking that I was in some trouble, I said, "Well—what's up?"

"Well, we'll get to that—but first, we heard that you weren't that religious, and we'd like to pray for you. Would that be all right?"

"Uhh...sure."

"Now, you're a big man, so I had to bring my *backup*,'" the man said, grinning and motioning to the 60+-year-old woman beside him.

"Okay, what should I do?"

"Just stand there, and we got it from here."

With that, he stood in front of me, and she stood behind me, and they reached forward and clasped each other's forearms and prayed.

"Oh Lord, please give the Big Fella here the strength to continue his hugging ministry and, uhh, high5ing people around the planet."

Reading my face when he said the word "ministry," he paused and then nodded at me and continued: "Big fella, I can see that you don't like the word 'ministry,' but it is what you are doing. So Lord, watch over him as he says things in a way that we won't. And, in turn, possibly positively touch people we could never reach. Do this so that the world can be a better place—Amen."

It was a brief prayer that left me filled with honor and nothing to say until the silence became awkward.

"What now?" I asked.

"Now—can we get one of these hugs that we keep hearing so much about?"

"Shit, yeah."

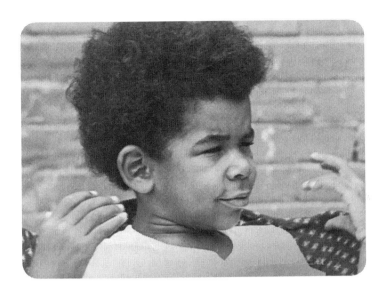

Fuck 'em

California State University, Northridge. 2015

Delivering the commencement address for Cal State, Northridge is one of my life's most esteemed achievements.

From thinking about what a student would want to hear, writing those life lessons down, and delivering my experiences to the students, their families, faculty, and staff: it was an inconceivably cool thing to happen to me.

The experience of it all was so grand that I got caught up in the moment and went "rogue" from my opening paragraph and asked the crowd if they wanted to know how good I felt.

Before they could answer, I ran down from the stage to high5 a few graduates seated in the first rows. It was a fantastic experience, but the most genuine and memorable moments came after my speech was over.

As I stood on stage in a receiving line with some CSUN dignitaries and professors, one student bypassed all of them to run up and embrace me. He said that he felt my energy in the very last row and hoped that he could be as happy as me one day. With that, he bounded down the steps, and we all yelled, "You forgot your degree." He smiled and said, "Oh yeah," ran back up the steps to retrieve it, hugged me again, patted me on the chest, and said, "Happy, man, happy!!" and then ran back down the steps.

After the ceremony, I milled around with the students and their families, soaking up the good vibes, and was approached by a woman who came over to me. "My father would like to speak with you," she said. I followed this woman until we reached a smiling old man in a wheelchair with his hand outstretched, ready to shake mine.

"Man, what a life, what a speech. Wow!" he said with great enthusiasm.

We began chatting, and he said that he'd been researching me during the rest of the commencement ceremony, and couldn't stop telling me how inspiring I was. Unable to match his spirit, I humbly said that I just hoped that the kids were inspired and got something out of my speech.

Without missing a beat, the man stopped smiling and said, "Man, fuck them kids. You know how kids are. They miss the point of everything—that's what they do. But you, you inspired me! I'm old, and I GOT IT!! Shiiiiiiiiiit, I'm ready to roll with you!"

As he said this, he popped a bit of a wheelie. I couldn't help but laugh, especially with his daughter standing behind him, rolling her eyes with embarrassment.

Afterward, I bent down to hug him, and laughingly said, "I get you, man: Fuck them kids."

Can I Afford to Stay On This Road?

Broke City, USA. 2015

Since September 11, 2001, I have been on my path to make the world a better place by offering hugs, high5s, and smiles through positive interactions.

It has been an enriching, one-of-a-kind journey, to be sure.

But years of one-way airfares, different bikes, gear, hotels, food, immunizations, lost wages, bills, etc., without a sponsor has consumed all of my savings.

All of this leaves me to wonder: No matter how fulfilling, should I even be on a road if I can't afford it?

Sometimes, I am so stressed about my lack of money that I can't think of anything else and need the hugs that I am freely giving out.

You may be reading this and think that you have no idea of that feeling, but you do. Imagine driving along on your favorite stretch of road, and suddenly, the "Low Fuel" light comes on.

Nothing has changed about the road; it is still a highly enjoyable stretch. But, as your grip tightens on the steering wheel and you nervously stare back and forth between the road ahead and the fuel gauge, everything has changed within you.

"Can I make it to the gas station?" you continuously think.

That feeling I've described is the knot that lives in my stomach a lot of the time. It is a strain that I try not to share for fear that viewing my struggle may dissuade others from going after their dreams.

But these were the thoughts that dominated my mind while I sat at an empty table at a book signing at the Cafe Gratitude in Santa Cruz, California. It wasn't that no one showed up for the book signing that got me down.

What got me down was that I had ordered some food when I arrived, figuring I would pay for it with some of the cash I would make from book sales. But, with no one there to purchase a book, I had no money. So I couldn't pay for my food when it arrived in front of me.

The food's aroma was mouth-watering, but the scent deflated me as I thought, "People around the world have told me I am doing something worthwhile, and I believe that I am doing something worthwhile in the world, but I can't afford to do this anymore. Shit, shit, shit, I can't even afford to eat."

I stared at the food, going through the calculations—which is quick and easy to do when you are broke—and concluded: "That's it. I'm out of the Hug and High5 business."

Though I concluded this quickly, the decision hurt.

It was as if I drove too far with the "Low Fuel" light blinking and was now stranded. So, there I sat at a table full of books, dispirited.

The line for the restaurant continued to grow, and by the time it wrapped around my table, people's stares felt like mocking screams, yelling, "You can't afford to be on this road!"

I tried not to let anyone see me biting my bottom lip or wiping away a tear, but I didn't think I was doing a good job.

So, I stood up to get some air.

When I did, I bumped into a man who was waiting for take-out food. "What's your book?" he asked.

I half-heartedly shared my story, but truth be told, I have no idea what I said. I just wanted to go outside and cry. After a few moments, he said, "My friend, I think you just sold a book, but I don't have $20—only my emergency $100."

Unable to pay for my food or break a hundred-dollar bill, I autographed the book and wrote my address.

"If you like the book, mail me the money. If you don't, then you just got something for free; either way, you win," I said and began to step outside.

"Wait, can you take a card?"

"Sure can," I said.

Thumbing through the book, he said that he would pay for his food first and then do our transaction. When he returned, he asked, "Hey, am I gonna get one of these famous Big Dave hugs that I keep seeing mentioned in this book?"

"Sure will," I said.

After chatting a bit more, he said, "This feels good...You know, I now know why I've been carrying this hundred...to give it to you."

With both of us touching the crisp bill, I said, "Sir, I am in no position not to accept this—so if this is just a gesture, then take it back."

"No, I mean it. Take it," he said.

I pocketed the money, he paid for the book with his card, and we shared a Big Dave hug, which led to more hugs and purchases from other patrons.

A short while later, the manager asked me why I hadn't touched my food, and after saying I couldn't pay for it, she looked at me like I was crazy.

"Who was charging you? You made all of our customers happy. Why should you pay?"

I share this story because I am not the only one driving on a highway toward a dream with one eye on the road and the other on a dwindling fuel gauge.

On the road with me are single parents, non-profit directors, artists, students, and others creating their own path. I've met many of them, and we've all shared stories like this.

Regardless of what your fuel gauge represents—funding, patience, peace, time, opportunity—please hang in there because help is out there, and it looks like the smile in this picture.

Hundred-dollar Hugs and High5s to you.

Not The Only Motherfucker

San Bernardino, California. 2016

After successfully planning and completing my Australian Hug and High5 Tour, I looked forward to doing an American version.

My American Hug and High5 tour was going to be my 4th time biking across the US with the ambitious plan of stopping to hug people in areas affected by violence.

The route would begin in San Bernardino, near where the mass shooting occurred and continue through Oklahoma City, Tulsa, Chicago, and other cities touched by violence and mayhem.

Before I go on, let me say this; planning cycling trips is always a lot of effort because you have to look over so many maps, alternate routes, cheap places to stay, and other details.

But basing a tour on acts of violence in America, was especially taxing because it involved me reading news stories of bloodshed throughout the country. And it didn't matter where I looked either: north, south, east or west—mayhem was everywhere and in every community. By the time I finalized my tour route, I felt absolutely ghoulish for all that I read.

I could say a lot, but I will sum things up by saying: basing a trip on heinous acts of violence was easy to do, too easy…and that's very sad.

We have to do better.

That aside, my tour plan was set.

> Fly to San Bernardino
> Rent a car to run some errands
> Take advantage of a great deal I found on a touring bicycle
> Begin pedaling east.

That may have been my plan, but things weren't feeling right from the very beginning.

I began to feel a bit run down days before my flight but attributed it to the long hours I'd been logging.

"I'll feel better," I kept thinking, but felt worse as time went on. I felt so bad that when someone hugged me at the airport, it actually hurt.

"It'll be OK, I'll just get some needed rest on the plane and feel better." I thought.

I didn't.

I felt worse.

When I saw three people waiting in the car rental line, my body ached so much that I felt too exhausted to stand. I sat down with the intent to rest a moment but ended up napping for 30 minutes. By the time I rented the car, I was reluctantly coming to grips with the fact that I was in bad shape.

It took an energy drink to feel upbeat enough to drive, but I didn't go to the bicycle shop as I originally planned. I just went to sleep.

The morning was better for me, but I quickly felt deflated upon discovering that the bicycle deal was nothing more than a bait-and-switch tactic to get people in the shop.

"Maybe this tour isn't going to work out," I thought.

My condition continued to worsen, as another disconcerting symptom came on; my lack of equilibrium. I could barely stand, and by the time I was using the maid's cart as a walker to get down the hallway- I had finally faced the fact: This tour was not happening.

After extending my stay, I stumbled back to my room and began to think of how to cancel my tour when my phone rang. It was my friend Caveman—yes, that is his nickname.

"Yo," I said.

"Yo man!" Caveman replied.

"What up?" I asked.

"What up?" he said—let me just say SO MUCH can be communicated through tonality among friends.

Hearing the distress in my voice, Caveman asked, "Fuck's wrong with you?"

I blabbered about not wanting to cancel my trip, and he cut me off, "Da fuck are you talking about?"

From there, I opened up about everything feeling awful, the bike shop's bait-and-switch, my balance, everything.

After a few moments of my whining, he said, "Ok, cancel it."

"Dude, I don't wanna cancel the trip."

Then Caveman unloaded, "Dude! Who the fuck is talking about canceling the trip? Look, man, for real, for real, no one cares about your cycling: that was your thing. As far as I am concerned, you have biked so much that it almost takes away from your story. This is what I see:

- You're broke yet travel the world.
- You curse all the time, and yet all types of people, parents, AND kids love you and WANT your black ass to keep talking.
- You are black and go anywhere you damn please, and if there is a problem—you say, 'C'mon man let's hug it out.'...and they actually hug you!!
- Shit man, you wrote a bestseller and can't even read."

I kan reed, by the way :)

And, he had more to say.

"You found a way around anything and everything that would've stopped me or anyone else. So cancel the bike portion of this trip and find a way to make this right and we'll all have more reasons to clown and admire your ass, and it will be for the same reason: Dave made some goofy-ass shit up, AND it worked."

Now dragged from my perch of self-pity, I said, "Wow, that's deep."

"Yo, man, you ain't the only deep motherfucker around here...now hang-up, bitch, and figure a way out of this shit," Caveman retorted, and then he hung up.

Postscript: It turns out that I had a sinus and ear infection. And, after resting for a few days, drove across the country—hugging over 1000 people.

Thank you, Caveman.

God Awful

California. 2016

I took a friend recovering from a surgical procedure to her first follow-up appointment and settled down in the waiting area.

My original plan was to check some emails on my phone but quickly abandoned that after discovering my battery was around 6%.

With nothing to do, I looked around the office for some magazines to read and didn't see any.

So I then looked to my right and began speaking to a woman also in the waiting area.

"How are you," I asked with a smile. She barely looked my way and nodded.

"I guess that this is where all of the support people gather," I cheerfully said. She rolled her eyes and put the book she was reading even closer to her face.

I figured that she didn't want to talk, so I sat in silence. After a few minutes, I REALLY DID have to clear my throat, and as soon as I did, she snapped, "Look, I do not do small talk!"

Shocked that she was now speaking to me, I said, "That's cool. I travel around the world hugging and high5-ing people, so I kind of do small talk for a living."

There was another distinct eye-roll accompanied by an ever-so-subtle groan as she put down her book and then said, "...what a God-Awful life you must have."

"I never thought so until you just said that," I said with a smile. She then rolled her eyes again and got up and left. Waiting for a moment after the door closed, the receptionist whispered, "What the hell was that about??"

"Not everyone is into hugs," I said with a smile.

I Am Not a Fashionista

Route 66. 2016

While stopping for gas somewhere along the historic Route 66, the couple working the register asked where I was going.

"To hug people," I said with a smile.

Both of them looked at me like I was insane, and explaining my story didn't seem to help change their expressions much, especially the guy's.

The woman was engaged in my story and kept asking questions about the places I visited and the people I encountered. The man, though, was different. Wearing a confederate flag hat and a gun on his waist, he just sat on his stool, staring at me, stone-faced.

Now, this was an interesting moment for me as there was a convergence of a few beliefs that have served me well.

- I believe that life is nothing more than a series of moments and what we do in those moments.
- Once you have achieved a good moment, then build upon it to create even more positive moments.
- As a motivational speaker, I believe that I can motivate almost anyone.
- As a hugger, I think that everyone wants one.

- Lastly, my Hug and High5 mission is about connecting all people by opening their minds a bit, and I believe you do that by having good moments with people.

So here I was with an opportunity to push all of my beliefs and boundaries in one shot. After speaking to the couple for about 15 minutes, I stepped out on faith and asked the guy for a hug.

"I don't hug men," he sneered.

Now once you step out on faith, you have to remain committed to it, so I said, "Shit, you ain't my first choice either! You ain't that cute," with a slight shrug, a bit an eye-roll, and a playful smirk.

I didn't get a sense that there was tension between the man and me, but his girlfriend seemed to think so. She piped right up: "Calm down...Shit, hug the man! He's just trying to make the world a better place."

With a "honey-do" tone dripping off every word and movement, the man agreed and said, "Aww, okay." Before he could walk around the counter to stand next to me, though, she spoke up again. She pointed to the Confederate flag cap atop his head and said, "And, for God's sake, take that damn hat off!"

I looked at him and told him not to take the hat off, saying, "You keep that on. You bought that—that's yours, man. I'm not a fashionista; I'm just a dude. Besides—we all hate someone, right?"

Pausing for a moment, he said, "We sure do," with a huge grin and laugh. And then we hugged...for a few moments longer than I usually do.

And I left, making sure to say, "y'all take care!"

When I tell this story, it's met with considerable backlash from people who felt I should have taken a stronger stance about the Confederate flag. You may feel that way too, so let me try to explain.

I don't believe that anyone ever changes their mind by being called a "dumb-ass." If that were the case, we would all be more competent folks after encountering a stern boss, head coach, mentor, or other leading figures.

I mean, it does work for some, but for the most part, it just makes people double down on whatever rhetoric they are espousing.

I believe that people eventually change their minds after having a few positive experiences with people they wouldn't have previously thought they could even interact with.

So, I did what I could to share a laugh, a smile, a moment, and even a hug with the man wearing a Confederate Flag hat with the hope that he will do the same thing as me: leverage our positive interaction into other positive interactions around the world.

After all, people are people, and if I want him to believe in my potential, then I have to believe in his.

I've Been Everywhere

Arizona. 2016

"Holy shit, there're black people here!"

Those are not the first words you'd think would be associated with a good story, but that is exactly how this story began.

Before that line was delivered, though, I asked a guy at my hotel for restaurant recommendations. Rather than tell me where to go, he told me where NOT to go and could have stopped talking right there because I had already decided.

The one place he told me not to go was a bikerv bar, and while I wasn't scared to enter the establishment, I wasn't a totally trusting fool, either.

I hedged things a bit by backing my car into a spot and leaving it unlocked so I could jump in and drive away quickly if need be. I didn't know quite what to expect when I entered the bar, so I grabbed a seat near the door and settled into people-watch.

The place was packed.

It was karaoke night, and people were milling around the DJ booth and choosing their songs from the song selection book.

And then it happened: the door opened wide, and a guy stepped in and bellowed those warm and welcoming words that every black man longs to hear: "Holy shit, there're black people here."

Always looking for the chance to have a smart-ass comment for someone, I immediately looked around the bar for other people of color and yelled back, "I'm only one person!"

"Yeah, but you're big enough for people," he said, putting his hands out to show the width of my shoulders in comparison to his.

"True," I said.

I had no clue what kind of guy this was but figured that even if he wasn't a good guy, everyone likes someone who offers them free shit. So I asked if he wanted a drink.

"Nah, man, but thanks. I got something already and just went outside for a smoke—what's your story?"

I began speaking of bike travels and such, but when I started talking about hugging people in different types of shelters and facilities, he took over the conversation.

He opened up about his childhood in foster care, being sexually abused, which led to his drug abuse and other issues.

"But," he said, raising his index finger to get my full attention, "I'm clean now and have been for eight years."

He wiped away a tear and muttered lowly: "You know hugs are power, right?"

"What?" I asked.

He shared with me that he'd done a lot of self-reflection throughout his eight years of sobriety. Now, with a clear head, he could see that he'd been in search of a hug in his younger days, not a high. He was "hunting for the hugs" that he didn't get as a child, and searching for the hugs he didn't get while being abused. He was looking for all of those embraces.

"Now"—again holding up his index finger—"I hug everyone: coworkers, bosses, family members, and even the people I used to get high with."

He said that he'd even hugged the people from the HR department at his job when he'd gotten reprimanded recently.

"They told me, 'You know that this meeting isn't a good thing, right?' and I told em, 'Yeah, but I still got a job—so it's all good.'"

With a tear in the corner of his eye, he said, "Hugs are the shit."

Soon it was his time to get up and sing his karaoke song, but instead of crooning, he talked—about me.

He took the microphone and stated that he wanted to introduce his "new friend" to the crowd, to which the bar crowd retorted, "Shut up and sing." He then yelled, with a cracking voice because he'd just been crying, "There are more important things than a song!"

"Shut up and sing," the crowd again yelled.

Looking at me but yelling at the crowd, he said, "You know what? Fuck it—I got you, man!"

Snapping open the karaoke songbook and rifling through its pages until discovering the song he wanted, he clutched the mic like he was about to belt out a song to a stadium filled with people.

"This one's for you, Big Dave. Now, I may fuck this up because I never sang this before, but it's yours." Then he did his best with Johnny Cash's "I've Been Everywhere."

...and, he did fuck it up, but it was still awesome.

As he sang, the bartender slid a drink across the bar and yelled over the music, "That was so NOT how I thought that was going to go."

"Me neither," I yelled back over the music.

"I've Been Everywhere"
by Johnny Cash
[for the record, I've been to 50 of the 80+ places listed]

I was totin' my pack along the dusty Winnemucca road,
When along came a semi with a high and canvas-covered load.
"If you're goin' to Winnemucca, Mack, with me you can ride."
And so I climbed into the cab and then I settled down inside.
He asked me if I'd seen a road with so much dust and sand.
And I said, "Listen, I've traveled every road in this here land!"

I've been everywhere, man.
I've been everywhere, man.
Crossed the desert's bare, man.
I've breathed the mountain air, man.
Of travel I've a-had my share, man.
I've been everywhere.

I've been to
Reno, Chicago, Fargo, Minnesota,
Buffalo, Toronto, Winslow, Sarasota,
Wichita, Tulsa, Ottawa, Oklahoma,
Tampa, Panama, Mattawa, La Paloma,
Bangor, Baltimore, Salvador, Amarillo,
Tocopilla, Barranquilla, and Padilla, I'm a killer.

I've been everywhere, man.
I've been everywhere, man.
Crossed the desert's bare, man.
I've breathed the mountain air, man.
Of travel I've a-had my share, man.
I've been everywhere.

I've been to
Boston, Charleston, Dayton, Louisiana,
Washington, Houston, Kingston, Texarkana,
Monterey, Faraday, Santa Fe, Tallapoosa,
Glen Rock, Black Rock, Little Rock, Oskaloosa,
Tennessee to Hennessey, Chicopee, Spirit Lake,
Grand Lake, Devil's Lake, Crater Lake, for Pete's sake.

I've been everywhere, man.
I've been everywhere, man.
Crossed the desert's bare, man.
I've breathed the mountain air, man.
Of travel I've a-had my share, man.
I've been everywhere.

I've been to
Louisville, Nashville, Knoxville, Ombabika,
Schefferville, Jacksonville, Waterville, Costa Rica,
Pittsfield, Springfield, Bakersfield, Shreveport,
Hackensack, Cadillac, Fond du Lac, Davenport,
Idaho, Jellico, Argentina, Diamantina,
Pasadena, Catalina, see what I mean-a.

I've been everywhere, man.
I've been everywhere, man.
Crossed the desert's bare, man.
I've breathed the mountain air, man.
Of travel I've a-had my share, man.
I've been everywhere.

I've been to
Pittsburgh, Parkersburg, Gravelbourg, Colorado,
Ellensburg, Rexburg, Vicksburg, El Dorado,
Larimore, Admore, Haverstraw, Chatanika,
Chaska, Nebraska, Alaska, Opelika,
Baraboo, Waterloo, Kalamazoo, Kansas City,
Sioux City, Cedar City, Dodge City, what a pity.

I've been everywhere, man.
I've been everywhere, man.
Crossed the desert's bare, man.
I've breathed the mountain air, man.
Of travel I've a-had my share, man.
I've been everywhere.

I've been everywhere.

It'll Be With You Shortly

Flagstaff, Arizona. 2016

While in Flagstaff, Arizona, I stopped to visit The Pay 'n' Take, a bar owned by my friend Scott. More than a friend, Scott is my brother and became that by bicycling across Africa, Asia, and North America with me. We hadn't seen each other in years, and he was so excited to see me that he began blasting old-school hip-hop and dancing atop the bar...Okay, maybe he wasn't that happy to see me.

The alcohol may have had something to do with things. Anyway, let me get back to the story.

Somewhere between Public Enemy's "Fight the Power " and EPMD's "Let tha Funk Flow," I began speaking with a woman and realized almost immediately that she was super wasted.

Through slurred speech, she asked what I was doing in Flagstaff, and when I told her about my trip's mission, she said that she wanted a hug.

169

I obliged her but when I did, a look of confusion came over her. I guess that she noticed my expression because she wrinkled her nose and quickly offered an explanation.

"I f_____"

"What?" I yelled over the music.

I am purposely leaving her words blank because I couldn't hear what she said, and repeated my question.

"What?"

Again, I heard, "I f_____"

I can only assume that she realized I couldn't hear her, because a look of understanding had replaced her confused expression and she loudly declared over the music, "IT WILL BE WITH YOU SHORTLY!"

"What will?" I asked, with my own look confused. But that look didn't last long, because "IT" did hit me, and "IT" was the stench of a stinky fart.

All hugs may be warm, but some are stinky too.

No Sex in the Champagne Room

Some Strip Club. 2016

After driving more than 300 miles one day, I wanted a drink but didn't feel like driving anymore—so I walked to the bar closest to my hotel, a local strip club.

It's true.

There was one problem, though: there wasn't any booze. The club had just (and I do mean just) lost its liquor license. I believe I passed the city official who had stripped (pun intended) the club's license as I was walking in.

Of course, the owner didn't notify me of this, so I ended up paying a cover charge in time to see most of the dancers and patrons talking about leaving the club.

So with nowhere to go and unaware of other bars nearby, I sat down, ordered a ginger ale that cost me seven bucks, and did what I always do: people-watch.

As I sat there, one of the few dancers who didn't leave approached me and said, "Hey!"

"Hey," I replied.

Turning to look at some guys leaving the club and at the DJ, who was packing up his stuff, she turned back to me and asked, "Why did you stay?"

"Because I've got nowhere else to go!" I said in my best Richard Gere, *An Officer and a Gentleman* voice.

Staring at me blankly because she didn't get the movie line reference, she said, "You want a dance?"

"Not now, but you can talk to me while I sip on this great non-alcoholic beverage that I paid an exorbitant cover for."

THAT joke she laughed at, and sat down and began talking about the club's mismanagement. She moved on to speak about other aspects of her life.

As she spoke, I began to do what I could to interject some advice and motivation, and as I did, she said, "Oh my God, you're actually listening."

"Uhh, yeah, it's kind of what I do," I said.

As we spoke, more patrons started leaving (I'm guessing that they weren't as big of a fan of over-priced ginger ale as I was), and another dancer asked what we were talking about.

"Oh my God, girl, he actually listens!" the first dancer proclaimed.

"For real?" the second dancer chimed.

That was all it took for the three of us to become engaged in a conversation that ranged from getting out of the stripper game to finishing college, other career paths, and other aspects of life.

Soon, though, one of the dancers got tired of yelling over the loud music and shouted, "Let's go somewhere where we can talk!!"

Before I knew it, the three of us were all in the champagne room, a curtained alcove where more private dances are supposed to occur.

As the conversation went on, another dancer looked through the curtain's break to see the three of us sitting down and asked, "What are you all doing?"

"Talking about life and shit," one dancer said.

"Cool," she said, as she walked into the champagne room, holding a glass of beer—I guess that liquor ban didn't apply to employees.

Now, I have to tell you that before the last dancer walked into the room, the two dancers and I laughed and had a fun and engaging conversation about making the best out of bad life situations.

But the energy that the last dancer brought in killed it.

She complained about everything: the liquor ban, her money, the weather, the customers, and whatever else she could. As she did, the two dancers and I just rolled our eyes.

She was soon dominating the conversation with her negativity, but when she began complaining, "No one does their job in life," I'd had enough of her.

Raising my finger to make my point, I said, "Really? Tell me about it. There are four people in this room, and no one is doing what they're supposed to. I'm not drinking, and YOU"—making sure to point at her—"ain't dancing."

"Neither are they," she said, taking offense and pointing to the other dancers.

"I came back here to talk to them. YOU…you barged in here!!"

The first two dancers started laughing and said, "You crazy!" while Bad-Energy-Betty left in a huff.

I talked to the other two dancers for a few more minutes, until the DJ announced that the club was closing due to no liquor. And then I left the champagne room…without having sex.

Postscript: One of the dancers took my advice and completed her associates degree program.

You Still Haven't

Flagstaff, Arizona. May 18, 2016

After my experience with the farter [see, "It Will Be With You Shortly"] and the air cleared a bit, I met a teacher from The Flagstaff Leadership Academy. They loved what I was doing and asked me to stop by their school the next day to speak with the students.

Now, seventh and eighth graders can be a tough audience, so I was shocked when one student stood up in the middle of my talk and proclaimed, "I want a hug now!"

I was even more shocked when every other student in the assembly looked upon our embrace and said, "Yeah, I want a hug too."

So there wouldn't be chaos, I said that we would hug after class.

After my talk, we all posed for a group picture and, to not infringe upon their recess time, I proposed that we all share in a group hug.

All I heard was a resounding chorus of, "No! I want my own!"

175

What happened next was unbelievable to me because all of these kids— and you know how chaotic kids that age can be—got in an orderly line for their hugs.

As the students patiently waited for their embrace, one teacher remarked, "I haven't seen anything like this."

"It's crazy to me, too," I said, adding that it was my birthday and like a great unexpected gift.

As word spread that it was my birthday, the kids swarmed me for one massive group hug and sang, "Happy birthday." It was a beautiful gesture that left me a bit weepy.

As I spoke with a teacher about it all, one student followed behind us and asked for another hug. After obliging him, the kid said, "Man, I've never hugged anyone famous before."

Not being able to resist a smart-ass comment, I just smiled and said, "Guess what? You still haven't."

To which he said, "Maybe not, but you're still cool."

The kid then asked for my business card and then, upon getting it, said, "Wait??!! IS THIS YOUR REAL PHONE NUMBER??"

"Yeah," I said. "It's the only phone I got," and continued speaking with the teacher. Moments later, my phone rang, and the kid said, "Oh my god, It's ringing!!"

Not used to this much excitement about getting my card or being looked upon as a celebrity, I dryly said, "That's what phones do, man."

The kid then excitedly said, "Cool!!" and walked off into the corner of the room. The teacher and I continued speaking until we heard the kid in the corner, talking on the phone.

"Hey, Dad, I'm at school...I know I am not supposed to give my number out to people, BUT I just met this cool man at my school and called him..." Before the kid went one word further, I looked at the teacher and said, "I think that it is time for me to leave...and trust that you'll handle this."

"Yeah, Dave. Who knew a hug was such a big deal!" he said with a laugh.

Two Honors, One Day

Chicago, Illinois. 2016

Because of budgetary constraints, I could only hug people from San Bernardino to Chicago, which meant that offering hugs at La Colombe Café in Chicago was my last stop.

It was the Friday before Memorial Day and, as with many of my other tour stops, I had nothing much to do but stand by a six-foot banner that read, "Ride. Hug. High5. Repeat" and offer what I could to make people smile.

There I stood, against the café wall, while the morning rush of coffee drinkers passed right by me. Most people in line high5'd me while looking at my laminated pictures and maps, and maybe asked a few passing questions about where I'd been.

One woman, though, who was with her husband and young daughter, asked some very pointed questions about my journeys.

She had traveled a lot and done a stint in the Peace Corps, and as we chatted, it quickly became apparent that we had covered a good portion of the globe between the two of us.

"But," she said while picking up her daughter and gently kissing her on the cheek, "that was all before I had her."

Ours was an interesting conversation that continued even after she and her family got their drinks, as we both began to shout out random places around the world to see if we had traveled there. With the line dwindling to just a few people, I moved over to sit with the family, and we continued exchanging stories about the people we had encountered and how they changed us.

As we spoke, the little girl played on her mother's lap. The woman said that she hoped her daughter would take after her and develop the travel urge but also be like me: strong enough to forge her own path and explore her own capabilities.

"It ain't easy," I said.

"For sure," she said, "but you're extremely confident, which helps everything."

"It does," I said.

We continued speaking about places we'd been and how those travels bolstered our sense of confidence.

Then this woman, whom I'd known for about 30 minutes or so, did something very honoring. She placed her daughter in my lap, looked her in the eye, pointed to me, smiled and said, "Meet your future."

After that moment, I figured my day couldn't get any better, so I decided to leave the café and head to the airport early to catch my flight home.

Once at the airport, I killed time by sitting in an airport bar, looking over my notes and pictures of my summer of hugs. Seeing all of the smiles and recalling all of the stories made me emotional, and I wept a bit.

I guess that my sniffiing and tear-wiping caught the guy's attention next to me because he asked if I was all right.

When I told him that I was okay and was just going home after an emotional summer's journey, it prompted a conversation. Moments later, he was looking at the pictures on my laptop with me and pointing, saying, "Tell me about that person . . . Now tell me about that picture."

As I shared my various stories, I could see that he was getting emotional at some points too, but I had to take a call and cut our chat short.

When I got off the phone, I noticed that the man was working on something and left him alone. He didn't say a word to me until they called for his flight to San Antonio. Then he asked me "Have you ever heard of the poem 'Abou Ben Adhem'?"

When I said I hadn't, he explained that it was a poem his mother would often read to him at bedtime when he was a child about an angel who stops by a child's room to do work on compiling a list of all the people who are going to heaven. In the poem, the child awakens to see the angel and asks what the angel is doing. After the angel tells him about the list the child asks if his name is on the list. The angel says no but maybe one day.

Time passes, and the angel stops by the child's room again.

The child again awakens and asks the angel if his name is on the heavenly rolls. After looking through the papers, the angel says, "Yes" and hugs the child.

After he gave his version of the poem, an entranced look overtook the man, and he began to recite the poem word for word.

"My God," he said, "I haven't even thought of that poem, or all of the stories that my mother would spin-off of it, in years."

Wiping a tear away from his damp eye, he stood up to gather his things for his flight and said, "Thank you for making me remember that poem and think of my mother...Dave, there is an angel out there with your name in his book. Bless you."

"Abou Ben Adhem"
By Leigh Hunt

Abou Ben Adhem (may his tribe increase!)
Awoke one night from a deep dream of peace,
And saw, within the moonlight in his room,
Making it rich, and like a lily in bloom,

An angel writing in a book of gold:—
Exceeding peace had made Ben Adhem bold,
And to the presence in the room he said,
"What writest thou?"—The vision raised its head,
And with a look made of all sweet accord,
Answered, "The names of those who love the Lord."
"And is mine one?" said Abou. "Nay, not so,"
Replied the angel. Abou spoke more low,
But cheerly still; and said, "I pray thee, then,
Write me as one that loves his fellow men."
The angel wrote, and vanished. The next night
It came again with a great wakening light,
And showed the names whom love of God had blest,
And lo! Ben Adhem's name led all the rest.

Everyone Likes a
Sharp Dressed Man

Cleveland, Ohio. 2016

The run-up to the 2016 presidential election was as contentious and divisive as I've ever seen. To do something to ease the nation's tensions, I formed a one-man third-party alternative to the Democrats and Republicans: The Hug-Party.

And to assert Hug Party's agenda of goodwill, I staged events at both the Democratic National Convention in Philadelphia and the Republican National Convention in Cleveland, Ohio.

The RNC was first that year and I appeared at a few locations throughout downtown Cleveland but staged my first appearance at The Rising Star Café right in the heart of the city.

The café opened at 6:30 that day and I was there, reporting for duty, just as if I were a paid employee.

Greeting every patron with hugs and good-vibes was a blast for me, and in my zeal to "leave no person unhugged" that morning, I embraced someone from Texas Governor, Rick Perry's staff. I know this because the former Governor himself appeared at the café sometime after 7:00 a.m.

While everyone else who entered the café was dragging and bleary-eyed after a late night of partying and in need of their morning cup of joe, Rick Perry appeared in the cafe like he was there for a modeling shoot.

I keep using the word "appeared" because that was exactly how it happened. In the glass-walled café, I was able to see everyone else as they approached the entrance, but Governor Perry was just—there.

Without a puff of smoke or the "Abracadabra!", Rick Perry materialized like a magician. Without even a hair out of place or ruffled in the least, he stared at me for a moment and said, "I hear you are the man that I am to talk to if I need a hug."

Shocked—because how often do you meet a governor who wants a hug and how alert he was—I stammered a bit and said, "Y-y-yeah."

"Great! Well, give me one," he said while giving me the old one-arm, half-a-hug.

Glancing through some laminated maps and pictures I had from my travels on the cafe tables, he said, "Man, you really have bicycled all over the world. That is something...Did you bike through Texas?"

As soon as I said, "yes," our conversation turned towards my favorite cities, cuisine, and stories I'd encountered in Texas, and he asked to take a picture with me. After the picture, he asked for another hug, this time giving me a full embrace and apologized for our chat's brevity. "I could talk all day, but have to be on one of the morning talk shows," he said.

And just like that, he was whisked into a waiting SUV.

When he left, one of the baristas said, "Wow, he was nice!" and asked if I'd ever met him before. When I said no, she said, "Wow" again and added, "that was really nice then."

I went back to hugging and high5-ing cafe goers and the next thing I knew, Governor Perry appeared in front of me again.

"Man, that really was a good hug. Can I get another?"

Dumbfounded that any governor would be asking me for another hug, I said, "W-w-well, sure!" I began trying to think of something interesting to say to him, but Bill Clinton's quote about Rick Perry was the only thing that came to mind: "He's a good-looking man."

With that being the only thing in my head after our hug was over, I looked at the Governor and said, "You really are a good-looking man."

My statement seemed to stop him for just a moment, and he looked at me and said, "Well, yeah!"

As he left for the second time, one nearby customer asked if I'd actually called him good lookin'. I said, "Yeah," and another customer said flatly, "Well, he is."

A One Man Organization

West Philadelphia. 2017

On my way to catch a train to work, I walked past an elderly woman who reached for my hand and asked, "Are you a nice man?"

Before I could even begin to answer, she looked up at me and said, "you are," and gave me her heavy book bag to carry.

When I gave her my arm to hold onto, she called me "a nice man" and shared that she was on her way to teaching the holy sacraments to some teens at Philadelphia's West Catholic High School.

We continued chatting another block or so, and I told her of my hugging people around the world.

She then asked if I was doing this as a part of any organization and when I said, "no," she stopped walking.

Taking my hand in hers, she stared up at me and said, "No, of course not, I can see that; you ARE the organization. That is just who...you..are!"

I asked to take a picture with her, and when she asked why, I said, "Because NO ONE is gonna believe this!"

And with that, meet Sister Sylvia, standing with me on the Philadelphia El platform.

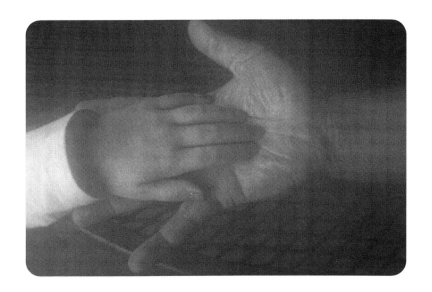

Say Anything

Mobile, Alabama. Christmas 2015

When I biked across the US for the second time, I pedaled through Alabama and gave service at Penelope House, a domestic violence shelter in the Mobile area.

Thanks to the executive director and passionate staff, my experience at the shelter was so informative and rewarding that I walked away pledging to return and do more one day.

You can read my full account of what happened in the "Faceless Angels" chapter of my book, *Traveling at the Speed of Life*.

Though it took me more than four years to honor my pledge, I returned to the shelter to have breakfast with the women and families staying there on Christmas Day.

Now pulling this off was no simple feat. My clients and friends donated so many feminine hygiene products, bed linens and gifts for the women and children that I couldn't fly. Instead, I rented a car and did my own 'Tour de Tampon' by driving more than 1,200 miles from Philadelphia to Mobile.

As I drove up to the shelter, there was nothing about the many cameras, perimeter fencing, or other necessary security measures that evoked emotions of peace on earth or other warm Christmastime feelings.

There was only darkness.

It wasn't until I passed through the two security doors and settled down in a common-room to meet some of the women and children, that things began to lighten up. Only as their expressions of stunned apprehension began to melt away and morph into smiles and hugs, did I start to feel some of the warmth and spirit associated with Christmas.

Not all of the looks I received were friendly. As the morning wore on, more mothers and their families entered the common area and, for many of them, the expression of surprise and fear never left their faces.

I told the staffer who was responsible for preparing Christmas breakfast that I would leave so as not to upset anyone, but she told me to stay.

"There's no way that I will let you drive all of this stuff down here from Philadelphia and be invisible and say NOTHING. You have to tell the people who you are NOW."

She then announced to everyone who I was, where I had been, and stressed the fact that I elected to be with their families on this holiday.

After that great icebreaker, the room warmed up to me and almost collectively said, "You came all this way just to have breakfast with us??"

"Yes," I said, and that opened the door for a great conversation over pancakes.

Afterward, one of the children wanted to play catch with a ball they'd received as a gift—but due to safety concerns and a chill in the air, we couldn't go outside. Instead, we elected to play catch in the shelter hallway that ran the length of the building.

As we played, the child threw longer and longer passes until we were throwing tight spirals almost the corridor's full length. Both of us got giddier and giddier with each toss, to the point that one woman admonished us to keep it down.

We both groaned, and I said, "Just a few more throws."

As I stood at one end of the hallway in front of a recreation room doorway, a woman seated on a sofa waved to grab my attention.

Having been admonished, I said, "I'm sorry, we'll keep it down."

"Oh, I don't care about that, it's a child's laughter—on Christmas, for Christ's sake," she said with an eye-roll in the direction of the woman who had asked us to be quiet. "No, I want to talk to you."

"Sure, give me a couple more throws." After those ball throws were over, I approached her and said, "What's up?"

"Listen," she said, touching my arm. "It's been a long time since my son has heard a good man's voice, and I'd appreciate it if you went in there and talked to him."

Looking inside the room, I could see her son alone, playing with a toy car and I said, "I don't know what to say."

She turned to me with watery eyes and said, "Say anything."

After embracing the woman, I walked into the room and looked down at her son who looked up at me bright blue eyes and said, "Hi!"

SEXY FAT!

Stillwater, Oklahoma. 2016

In Stillwater, Oklahoma, I staged a Hug Party at Eskimo Joe's, a popular eatery on the Oklahoma State campus. Because of a few radio interviews, the event turned out to be pretty successful, with many people showing up to get hugs. But one guy who attended had other ideas.

He wanted to give me a hug.

I could feel this guy's good-natured energy as soon as he hit the door, especially because when he yelled, "Big Dave!! I love what you're doing and just want to say that I am going to go over there [pointing to an open spot at the bar] and get my eat on and AFTER THAT, we are gonna get to huggin'!!"

What could I say but, "Ok."

You would think that I wouldn't forget this guy with all of his energy, but I did. About 30 minutes later, he was standing in front of me and saying, "Let's get to hugging!!"

I usually am the one that initiates an embrace, but as I said, this guy had other ideas. When we hugged, he had both arms wrapped around my ribcage and held on for a few moments. But then, he quickly moved his arms lower and shifted his weight to drop his hips a bit. Noticing this, I said, "what's going on??"

As if he was expecting my question, the guy excitedly exclaimed, "It's Happening, Man!!!... You've picked up the world, and now I am picking you up!!!"

His actions were a total shock to me and as a big dude, I just knew that he was going to drop me. I braced myself for the worst and quickly scanned the room to predict where we were going to fall and what furniture we were going to break. But it didn't happen. As soon as he swept me off my feet, he placed me back down.

He stepped back and smiled only to see a look of surprise still on my face and yelled, "Hey man, I may be fat, but: I AM STRONG!! I'm what you call SEXY-FAT!! I can move brotha!!"

"Yes, tha fuck you can," I said.

Hugging a Bad-Ass

Cleveland, Ohio. 2016

With the 2016 election cycle being one of the more embittered ones that I have seen, I decided to sprinkle in some good vibes by staging a Hug Party at the Republican National Convention in Cleveland, Ohio.

Most people don't know how to reply when I request to come and hug people, but the Rising Star Coffee Roasters manager did.

"If you are coming here to promote peace, calm, and goodness, you are more than welcome."

Once there, I happened to meet former US Navy SEAL and *Lone Survivor* author Marcus Lutrell. I recognized him immediately, and my first thought upon seeing this tall man was, 'How did short-ass Mark Wahlberg play this big mother-fucker?!'

Marcus was super cool to meet and as interested in my story as I was interested in his.

Most people want to know where I have traveled in life, but Marcus was different. He wanted to know where my mind goes when I am traveling the world all by myself and how I stay motivated while on my path. Our chat between sips of coffee was highly engaging because the topic of "how a person thinks" is fascinating.

Marcus shared a vivid memory of being a teenager in West Texas and driving a beat-up truck with a broken tape deck and a weak radio signal.

"Sometimes, I would just drive in silence for hours thinking about all kinds of things...what about you?"

"Shit, I'm just a happy-go-lucky dude who believes that wherever your mind is going —up or down—solitude only gets you there faster. So, when I return from a bike trip or car trip or goodwill travels, I'm just happier and go- luckier," I said.

"I like that. I LIKE THAT!" Marcus replied, sounding a bit like Hulk Hogan in tonality but with an air of legitimate Badass-ness mixed in.

After talking for 15-20 minutes, Marcus asked for another hug before he had to go. After embracing, he said, "You be safe out there, brother. Hugs are powerful, but you still need to be careful."

"You be careful out there too," I said.

It's incredibly uncommon to meet a celebrity, and even more unusual to have that celebrity be cool but that is what happened.

Here's to hoping you meet a cool celebrity as well.

Promises, Promises

Philadelphia, PA. January 1, 2017

To have 2017 begin on a good note for Philadelphia's citizens, I elected to offer hugs, high5s, and good vibes to people during the city's busiest event: the annual New Year's Day Mummers Parade. Regardless of the weather conditions, the parade draws revelers from all over the region to watch string bands strut their stuff down the city's most prominent street, Broad Street.

That year, the famous Kimmel Arts Center located on Broad Street, opened their doors to people for family-friendly entertainment like face painters, jugglers, clowns, and now huggers. Revelers, families, and people looking to escape the intense winter's chill packed the center.

195

Now, let me pause and say there are two types of people I regularly encounter: The person who looks at the map of everywhere I've hugged and says, "Wow, look at all the places you've been!"

And, the person who looks at the same map states: "Jeez, look at all of the places you have to go."

The little old lady in the picture is the latter.

She looked over her glasses and squinted over my "Hug-map" and began asking about where I had been. After answering all of her questions, she looked back at the map and said, "Ok...I will hug you, BUT...only if you promise to go to Israel. You need to go there, and they need to see you; you need each other. I can feel it."

The woman then went on and on about how beautiful Israel is, how I would love it and how they would love me.'

"I promise," I said.

"Ehhh, I don't know," she hedged. "I promise," I said with a smile.

"Ok, come and get it," she said with open arms and an even bigger grin.

This isn't the end of this story because this woman kept walking by my table, yelling, "Remember, you promised me," over the crowd noise.

Over the next few hours, she passed me a countless number of times yelling, "Remember your promise," each time.

But later on, she returned with a little man in tow and said, "I brought you someone else to hug, but you have to promise him too. Anyone can say something to one person, but you HAVE TO follow through if you promise two people."

I smiled and went to hug him, but he stopped me with a stiff-arm. "You didn't promise yet," he said.

"I promise."

"..To whaaaaat??" The old lady chimed in. "To go hug people in Israel."

"NOW, we hug again," she said with a look of self-satisfaction and joined the man for a group hug.

It took over two years for me to honor my word and, to be honest, I forgot all about this woman and my promise until I was returning from a hug trip I eventually took to Israel.

I was scrolling through past pictures to send to a reporter and happened upon her picture and thought, "Holy shit, I DID love Israel, and they DID love me. She was right."

You can read some Israel hug stories later on in the book but know this: it's essential to keep your word in life...especially to little old ladies—they know what they're talking about.

Love & Cigarettes

Smith Center, Kansas. February 13, 2017

Within hours of Donald Trump's election on November 8, 2016, it seemed like the country erupted in all types of protests.

Months later, in January, the protests were still going strong, with no ending in sight. One of the older members in the gym where I worked had just woven his way through one of these protests, took off his hat and gloves, plopped down in a chair and loudly exclaimed in exhaustion, "Can someone save a cat from a fuckin' tree and just give me some good news to read about, for Christ's sake?"

Something about the drained expression in this man's eyes got to me, so I took it upon myself to create some good news by going to the "heart" or nation's geographic center for Valentine's Day 2017 to hug and high5 people to give the country the uplifting story it needed.

Lebanon, Kansas, is the geographic center of the nation. With a population of 195 people, the town is so small that it closes up at night, leaving me to have dinner at Pooches Steakhouse in Smith Center, the next city over.

The restaurant was empty, except for a bartender and one patron named

Ron, who assumed I was passing through town. He asked where I was going and seemed dumbfounded when I told him that I came there to stage a Hug Party. After explaining my story, he said nothing for a few moments and then just opened up about wanting a hug from only one person but being unable to get it.

You see, Ron's wife recently passed away. It was especially painful for him to even think about Valentine's Day because their 54th wedding anniversary was just days earlier, and he was sorely missing her.

He stopped himself in the middle of speaking and asked, "You aren't a doctor, are you?"

"No, why?"

"I don't like doctors, and I want to like you."

Smoking and reeking of cigarettes, he said that he didn't like doctors "... because they took my wife."

When I asked him to explain, he opened up about his wife's cancer diagnosis, the pain, and the loans to try and save her. He also talked about their brief move to Texas to be closer to a specialist.

Holding my forearm and staring over my shoulder at a corner of the empty restaurant, he said, "I believed them—the doctors. I did everything they said to keep her alive. I listened to everything that they said, and she died even faster than the prognosis . . . They took my wife . . . They took my life. They took my wife, my life...And now they're telling me not to smoke?! To hell with that—whatever they tell me to do, I do just the opposite," he said. "I just want to be with my wife again."

Looking at Ron stare off and listening to his story in a restaurant decorated with red hearts, and Cupid's arrows was a challenge. I tried changing the subject by asking him what he kept staring at.

"Our table," he said.

Taking out his phone to show pictures of himself and his wife dining at their table, I couldn't help but notice his smile. I asked if he wanted to have a drink and carry on our conversation at their table.

"Yeah," he said, and soon we were talking and laughing like old friends, his smile growing with each story told.

When I asked for a picture with him, he refused, saying that he didn't want people to see his tears but he hugged me and said, "Keep doin' what you're doin', big man; It's good. Now eat your steak."

Promises, Promises II

Lebanon KS. 2017

When I called Lebanon, Kansas mayor, Rick Chapin, about staging a hug-party in his city, I could hear a lot of hammering in the background. It turns out that in addition to his mayoral duties, Rick is also a general contractor.

He was on the job at the time, and I could hear him cover the phone and say, "hold on a sec," to his crew. After hearing some 'shushing' in the background, he returned the phone and said, "...you wanna do WHAT, now??"

Usually persuasive on the phone, Rick sounded wholly unconvinced by anything I said. When I added that I could provide him with many press links to prove my legitimacy, he skeptically said, "Well, you're just gonna have to send ALL of that over to me."

Keenly focused only on getting permission to stage an event in his town, I never considered the high degree of skepticism I sensed from Rick until after my Hug Party. That night, I got the opportunity to thank Rick right before the town council convened but not before he spoke first.

Seated in a folding chair in a double-wide trailer that serves as the city's main municipal building, I listened to Rick standing behind me with his hand on my shoulders. He explained to everyone that, because Lebanon is the geographic center of The United States, he gets many calls from politicians and companies that want to do events and promotions there.

"They always promise what they're going to do for our town but rarely deliver... and often just want to use the town as some sort of punchline...so I asked Dave: "What are you really gonna do when you come here?""

Looking down at me, Rick said, "Do you remember what you told me?"

"Yeah," I said.

"Well, why don't YOU tell 'em exactly what you said."

"Exactly??"

"Yeah...EXACTLY"

I looked up at him and said, "I told you that I was just coming here to hug and high5 a motherfucker: that's it."

The crowded trailer erupted with laughter, and Rick looked around and yelled, "EXACTLY!!...and that is EXACTLY what he did! You got a mouth on you, man...but this town and this world need more people that keep their world, Dave. This world needs YOU."

After that, I hugged, and high5'd everyone in the trailer.

Let that be a lesson to you if you're going to keep anything: KEEP YOUR WORD.

It's All Over You

Rawlings County, Kansas. 2017

My 2017 Valentine's Day Hug and High5 Party at the nation's geographic "heart" in Lebanon, Kansas went better than I could have dreamt. In just one day, I was able to embrace 105 people in a city that only has 195! Among the people that I embraced, two were over 100 years old and one guy shared that he drove to Lebanon from Wyoming, over 400 miles, to get a hug.

It was a fantastic day.

As I drove through the night to the Denver airport to fly home, I relived all of the heartwarming moments. But, as I left a gas station in Rawlins County, Kansas and saw a white SUV about to pull away, something occurred to me. Out of all of the people I hugged, I didn't embrace a cop.

Acting purely on "hug-instinct"—it exists, at least within my spirit—I whipped my car around in front of the truck like I was on Starsky and Hutch, and yelled, "Whoa, whoa STOP!"

The truck abruptly slammed on its brakes. Before the cop could open his door, I was out of my car and standing by his driver's side door, excitedly saying, "Dude, I gotta hug you!!"

"What??" The officer yelled with widened eyes.

Seeing the expression of shock on his face made me stop dead in my tracks and take full account of my surroundings and circumstances. Here I am, a black man yelling at a cop in the middle of Kansas about wanting a hug. "What the fuck did I just get my black ass into?" I thought.

I immediately raised my hands a bit, lowered my register, and calmly said, "Hey man, I'm going around the world hugging people and..." I quickly and calmly explained my story, while backing away and ended with, "it's JUST a hug; no bullshit."

There was silence for a few moments, and then the cop smiled and said, "Hey man, It's ok. It's all over you."

Puzzled, shocked, and thinking that something was actually all over me, I kept my hands up but looked down at my clothes.

"What's all over me??' I said.

"Goodness...Something...Shit, I don't know, but it's all around you. Of course, we're gonna hug," he said with a big smile.

With that, the sheriff got out of his SUV, gave me a big hug, and then we took pictures with each other's phone.

Crazy, but oh so true.

How Do You Say "Hug" In Albanian?

July 3, 2016

While sitting outside of a cafe, I noticed that a man seated next to me kept fidgeting and looking around. After asking if he needed any assistance, I learned that he was okay and only killing time waiting for his daughter. I also learned that he was from Albania and didn't speak English well at all.

Because so many people have helped me bridge language barriers throughout my travels, I now feel obliged to return the favor and help others. I began downloading a translation app on my phone but didn't want to sit in silence, so we started talking. Communication was challenging, but we were able to do it using a mixture of his broken English, my body language, and our facial expressions.

Through that, I learned that his daughter was a doctor, his grandson was a year old, and his son-in-law was an ass...or a 'gomar' in Albanian.

We laughed a lot at that one.

We communicated as much as we could for about 30 minutes before I had to go. Before leaving, I gave him my business card and got him a cinnamon roll to snack on while he was waiting. His smile beamed towards me as he placed my card in his pocket and hugged me. After our embrace, he held onto my upper arm and put his hand on my chest atop my heart and bellowed, "Good."

I walked away from the cafe, thinking that I would never see or hear from him again, but that wasn't the case. Around 10 PM that evening, I got a call from a woman with a thick accent saying, "I'm sorry for calling so late, but my father is making me call you to say 'Thank You' for your kindness today."

To this day, I receive a text from him on every major holiday, always wishing me the best.

David Martin ✔
@FOX35David

⚙ ⚲ Follow

RETWEET if u need a hug. Big Dave from
DavidHaleSylvester.com will be @DrPhillipsCtr
memorial site Tuesday. #FOX35

A Hug Instead of
a Parking Ticket

Orlando, Florida. 2016

After the Pulse Nightclub massacre, I went down to Orlando, Florida, to offer what hugs and support I could, but was nervous about it because this was my first hug venture so close to the actual event. Most times, I wait a week or so afterward, so I don't get swept up in the politics of anything.

My anxiety eased considerably though, when David Martin of Fox 35's "Good Day Orlando" heard my story and agreed to do a spot on my actions.

My on-air time was for 6:30 a.m. at a memorial established at The Dr. Phillips Performing Arts Center. I could feel the memorial's intense emotion even while I was circling the Center in my rental car looking for a parking spot.

With each pass, I noticed more about the block-long green space between

Orlando's City Hall and the arts center. It was filled with banners, flowers, balloons, candles, pictures, and signs memorializing the many slain souls.

And with each pass, I became more mournful and saddened for the Orlando community. Eventually, I gave up and decided to park in a tow-away zone figuring that I wouldn't get a ticket that early in the morning.

Before going on air, I walked around the memorial. Each person I encountered had an intense and harrowing story. The first person I embraced was a woman who was supposed to be with her friends in the club but opted to nap first. To hear her describe waiting in line to get in the club just as the first shots rang out and talking about one of her friends being killed was chilling.

"Why? Why?!" she sobbed.

Later, I met two other people who said that they were at the club that night. After hearing their detailed account of the evening, I was ready for a hug myself.

I was so ready for an embrace, that I gave Fox's David Martin the biggest hug that I could muster in the middle of my segment.

Afterward, I milled around looking for other people to embrace—and that's when three official-looking black SUVs rolled up and stopped right behind my car. None of the vehicles stirred for a moment, and then all at once, a bunch of security guards and very serious-looking people stepped out.

"I'm gonna get a damn ticket," I thought.

Someone pointed over toward the cars and said that it was Florida's Governor, Rick Scott, and I thought, Shit, I'm gonna get towed!

As the Governor made his rounds with his staff, two of his security guards stood dutifully by their vehicles—and my car. I wanted to move it but refrained because I didn't want to announce that I was illegally parked. So I just drifted over by them hoping that they wouldn't tow me.

Even though the Governor's presence generated a bit of a buzz, the memorial's overall tone remained quiet and still. So it was kind of startling when a woman's voice sliced through the solemnity of it all.

"He's here?!"

I ignored the woman, assuming that she was one of the Governor's constituents, but I soon noticed that the woman wasn't anywhere near the Governor. She was standing with the Fox 35 reporter behind me. Looking around for who or what she was excited by, I caught David's eye. He nodded my way and pointed toward the woman.

I mouthed the words, "I don't know her" to him, and he mouthed the words, "She knows you."

I looked at the woman, and before I could even really greet her, she said, "Oh my God, I've been following you since 2008."

Stunned, "What?" was all I could say.

It turned out that this woman had been following me via social media ever since I wrote an ESPN piece in 2008. "Your intensity for life and living just leaped out at me," she said.

She said that she'd always wanted to meet me and thought it was "so cool" I had pivoted from just bicycling continents to now driving through areas touched by violence and mayhem.

She said she felt that meeting me would only occur "if something extraordinarily bad happens." She then paused.

"Oh my God—it happened. Something extraordinarily bad happened, and you are here—doing what you do."

Tears began streaming down her face as she collapsed into my arms, and in between her weeping, all I heard was, "I'm so glad to meet you (but) I am so sad to meet you. I am so sad...I'm so sad."

The Pride of New Canaan High

Orlando, Florida. 2016

The memorial for the 49 people killed and 53 wounded in the Pulse Nightclub massacre was highly impactful.

Established in a block-long green space between Orlando's City Hall and the Dr. Phillips Arts Center, the area was filled with flowers, balloons, candles, keepsakes, and pictures that made you feel mournful and wonder how such a monstrous act could ever occur. Though filled with people, no one spoke above a whisper and the only sound you heard was the weeping of others. The memorial was intense.

It was especially intense for me and took me out of my comfort zone because I do not do well with extreme quiet. And I was especially out of my comfort zone when I embraced a man named David.

While still clinched, he loudly wailed that there was "a target on his back" because of his lifestyle. I could actually feel the pain and anguish within his body and wanted to do something—anything—to offset it.

Acting on instinct, I said, "There isn't a target on your back because of your lifestyle."

As soon as I said that, David's body stiffened up a bit. While stepping out of the hug and wiping away a tear, he pleaded, "There isn't? Well, what is it then?"

Totally not expecting him to call me out, I looked at him, took a bit of a breath, and said, "It's that goofy-ass shirt you're wearing." Looking like he'd just been splashed with a bucket of ice water and speaking with a tone of stunned disbelief, David said, "Uhh, what?"

"Dude, everyone knows that no one likes New Canaan and that all the cool kids go to the school across the river."

My words just laid there in space for a moment.

Then David grabbed the bottom of his crimson and gold New Canaan High Athletic Department T-shirt. He looked down briefly, then up at me, and said, "How the hell do you know that?"

Again, called on my statement, I said, "I don't…I just know that there is always a cooler school on the other side of the river, and took a chance."

David's eyes got big for a few moments, and then he laughed—and laughed—and laughed some more. David's laugh pierced the deafening silence and pain that enveloped the area and was a welcoming sound.

"Oh my god, I shouldn't be laughing," he said as he hugged me again.

"Laughter is life," I said and added that we weren't laughing about anything that was happening but just trying to get through this awful moment.

With that, David, his cousin, and I sat down for a while to talk a little, cry a bit, laugh some more and hug a lot.

We Think What We See

Lebanon, Kansas. 2017

After the 2016 Presidential election, I believe that no matter what side you were on, the only thing we all agreed upon was that there was tension in the air.

At least, that's what I felt.

To create a good news story for people to read about, I staged a Hug Party at the nation's geographic heart on Valentine's Day.

Where, exactly, is the heart of the nation, you ask?

You have two options: the geographic center of the contiguous United States in Lebanon, Kansas, or the geographic center of the United States—given Alaska and Hawaii—in Belle Fourche, South Dakota. For a few reasons, mostly fiscal, I chose Lebanon, Kansas, and am glad that I did.

Upon reaching the town library where I was appearing, I saw one of the coolest signs ever hung on the door:

HUGS AND HIGH5S

2–5 PM

FEBRUARY 14th

DAVE SYLVESTER

The event was a total success, and at the end of the day, I spoke with the town's librarian while cleaning up. At one point, I asked her what she wanted me to say to people when I spoke with them about my experience in the "flyover states."

"For starters," she began as she pushed in the reading carrels' chairs, "tell them that we hate that term: flyover states."

"And after that," she concluded, "I guess just tell them that; we think what we think because we see what we see. Yeah, I guess that's it."

There was a depth within the simplicity of her words that made me repeat them in my mind: we think what we think because we see what we see. The phrase stuck in my head, and with nothing to do but begin a long drive to the Denver airport, I really tried to see things as she did.

As I walked from the double-wide trailers that served as both a wing of the library and Lebanon's City Hall, I first took note of all the one-story buildings and the street's width that allowed people to park perpendicularly. I obviously saw all of these things before entering the building, but was now trying to focus on them and connect how seeing them would change my thought process.

I didn't have any of this in Philadelphia, especially the peace and quiet, I thought.

It was a great mental exercise that had me thinking a lot, and I continued with this as I went to a gas station convenience store. Before exiting the car, I noticed that the person next to me had left their car running because it was so cold.

With "We think what we think because we see what we see" emblazoned on my mind, I took a deep breath, opened my car door, closed it behind me and hesitantly walked into the store.

I wasn't getting much, just road snacks, but I was a nervous wreck.

I kept looking down the aisles through the big front window at my unlocked and running car. I ran to the back of the store to get a bottle of water and then ran back to the front to peek at my car. And, as I stood at the sandwich counter, I nervously kept glancing out the window. My sneak-peeks continued, and once at the register, I kept leaning to one side to glance over the cashier's shoulder to look at my car. The cashier became concerned.

After turning his head to look behind him, he turned back to look at me and said, "Uhh, you all right, man?"

"Uh, yeah. It's just that it's my car—the engine is running," I said. The cashier stopped ringing me up to turn around entirely.

He examined the lot, turned to face me, and plainly said, "ALL of the cars are running."

I don't know if he was being a smart-ass or just opening my eyes to facts. But he stood to the side to give me a full view of the lot filled with empty cars and their engines running.

Now shaken from just being consumed by the view of only my stuff, I took note of the exhaust fumes contrasting against the dusky Kansas sky, and said, "Oh yeah, I really see that now,"

What do you see?

What do you think?

A Hug Instead of a Parking Ticket II

The Deep South. 2017

On my 48 state, 77 day, Big Dave Hugs America Tour, I got a parking ticket in one southern state capital city.

Feeling that it was bound to happen, I laughed when I saw the ticket and left it on the car and walked around the city.

While walking around, I encountered a police officer who said, "Hi." I began to engage him in some small talk, and he shared that he hadn't traveled that much beyond the state lines throughout his life.

"It's a beautiful world; you should go see it," I said and asked for a hug and a picture. He obliged me on both, and when I put the camera down, I saw that he wasn't a cop after all but someone from the parking authority. I laughingly said, "Oh shit, you just wrote me a fuckin' ticket!"

He bristled at my words, but I smiled and quickly added, "Cuz, it's all good. I fucked up—I will pay the fine. Really, it's cool."

As I smiled, so did he, and he began asking me more questions about the world and the people I've encountered.

After a few minutes, he asked, "Where's that ticket?"

"On the car."

"Go get it."

With that, I ran over to the car and handed over—what turned out to be two tickets.

"What are you going to do?" I asked.

"Take care of 'em."

"I didn't ask you to do that."

"Yeah—and I bet no one asked you to take the effort, money and time to go around the world and do what you do. Now, don't worry about this and just go on and do what you do and enjoy your stay here."

Afterward, he asked for another hug but asked that I not post his picture or any other identifiers with this story.

I am obliging him that courtesy, but it did happen, and it is a great story.

Thank you.

Waiting For
the Punchline

Leflore County, Mississippi. 2017

After hugging people all night at Jackson, Mississippi's Hal and Mal's Blues Bar as a part of my Summer of Hugs Tour, I got off to a late start the next morning. While getting dressed, a breaking news story flashed across the screen: A military transport plane crashed—killing 16 service members in the middle of Mississippi's Leflore County.

My tour's itinerary had me driving to hug people in New Orleans that morning, but I thought about all of the first responders who would have to comb through the fiery wreckage on this hot, July Mississippi morning.

Those guys are going to NEED a hug, I thought.

With that, I made a last-second change to my plans and began driving to Leflore County. Cutting through miles and miles of farmland, my two-hour drive from Jackson to Leflore County was peaceful, but I had to figure out where to go once I got there.

I drove around for a bit and saw nothing, so I waited on the roadside, figuring that a downed military plane would mean "official traffic" of some sort. After about a ten-minute wait, a car sped by, and I pulled out to follow it.

Good idea, right?

Wrong.

I followed the speeding car right to a nearby gas station. When I asked the people working there if they were aware of where the crash site was, they gave me a strange look and just said, "Somewhere around here."

Okaaaaaaaaaaay, I thought.

My next bright idea was to look to the sky and hope that some signs would appear.

It did, in the form of a crop duster.

They'll know where a plane went down, I thought.

Driving with one eye on the road and the other on a biplane darting along the horizon, I zigzagged through Leflore County's fields until I reached the crop duster's landing strip. Once there, I introduced myself to the pilot, hugged him, got a tour of the plane, met the other guys who worked there and found out where the plane went down.

Success.

Understandably, I couldn't get to the actual crash, so I went to a community center serving as the command center for all the local, state, and federal agencies involved in combing through the wreckage.

With news vans from local stations and Louisiana and Arkansas parked all over the place and their reporters standing outside giving "up to the minute updates," the center was teeming with activity.

Inside, people from the Red Cross and other agencies were bringing in water and food cases for the first responders, and others were rushing around with clipboards and speaking into radios. The building was alive with activity, and there I stood there in stark contrast—wearing shorts, sandals, and holding a "Big Dave Hugs America" sign, looking for someone to embrace.

Getting a hug ain't gonna be easy, I thought.

The first people I approached were military guys who had just come from the crash site and were still wearing all of their gear. They smelled like something burnt, and when one of them took his hat off, sweat poured from him as I have never seen before. When I said what I was doing, they just looked past me at a cooler filled with ice and water and said, "Uhh, yeah—go sit over there."

So there I sat, just like on the side of the road, waiting for an opening. This time an opportunity came in the form of food.

When the volunteers came in with trays of food, I followed them right to where they were setting up and waited for people to hug.

I didn't have to wait long; soon the room filled up with more than 50 guys from ATF, NTSB, and Fish and Game, as well as the state and local police who had come from the crash site and were looking for food, water and an air-conditioned place to sit.

I stood in the corner of the room while people entered the room and guzzled water and Gatorade and scarfed down food—but when some of the guys started speaking about specific things at the crash site and were beginning to debrief, I spoke up and stated my purpose.

After I spoke, one guy yelled out to me, "Are you a cop?" and another yelled, "Aren't you ex-military?" and another said, "Are you a fireman?"

I yelled back, "no" to each query and said, "No, I am just a dude." Silence.

"Wait—you're just a dude that hugs people?"

"Yup."

One of the men said, "I, personally, am not a hugger, but I do believe that I speak for every man in here when I say that I will take every high5 you got."

Before he could even really finish the sentence, I began making my way around the many tables and high5-ing each law enforcement member. Before leaving the room, I told the guys that I would sit in my car in the parking lot if they needed a hug. I spent about an hour in the lot and then began my drive to Louisiana, the next state on my tour. As I drove out, I stopped at every state trooper who was blocking the wreckage road. Most of the officers just looked at me and gave me a high5, but one officer was different. As I approached his cruiser with my sign, he just yelled, "Holy shit. you're really real."

"Uhh, yeah."

"You don't understand—they've been saying on the radio that there was a big dude offering hugs to the guys, and I thought that it was a joke. Shit, I have been sitting here waiting for the punchline."

I looked to my left and right and said, "I'm it."

With that, he got out of the car and hugged me.

What's Bigger Than a Dream

Mobile, Alabama. 2017

When traveling through Mobile Alabama, I had lunch at Callaghan's Irish Pub with Tonie Ann Torrans, the executive director of Penelope House, a domestic violence shelter in the area with which I have done work.

Tonie has been a supporter of my story for years, and it was good to catch up with her. Right before we ate, she encouraged me to stand up and tell the bar about my ambitions to hug America that summer. After speaking to the popular eatery, one woman stood up almost immediately and waved me over.

Before I reached her, she excitedly exclaimed, "I am a 77-year-old cancer survivor and grandmother, and I had a dream about something like this. I've been telling people all about my dream and saying that there needs to be something out there like this to bring people together."

She paused briefly, wrapped one of her arms around me, and began to well up with tears and emotion. She then patted my chest, right above my heart, and said, "But with your backstory, you are so much bigger than my dreams—look at you—you're so much bigger than my dreams. You are an undeniable man—simply undeniable."

With that, she nudged me a bit and urged me to embrace everyone in the restaurant— "And don't be denied. Hug everyone. The world needs you!"

Ain't that America

I-35, Texas.

Meet Bicycle Bill, a homeless man I first noticed while driving on I-35 North out of Austin.

It was a hot morning that would become an even more blistering day, and Bill was slowly bicycling along towing a small bike-trailer. I saw a thick sweat line on his shirt and thought of how many times I've done that.

*"That dude is me...*I'm gonna offer him a ride," I thought.

Due to some road construction, there was nowhere to pick him up. But about a half a mile later, I pulled over to the shoulder of the road and waited on the side of the sun-drenched road. Waiting outside of the car, I stood and thought, "this guy is going to cook out here in this heat."

I watched the cyclist pedal along, oblivious to my presence until he was about ten yards away. That's when he abruptly stopped and just stared at me. I waved for him to keep coming towards me, but he didn't budge and just stood there, shielding his eyes from the morning sun.

Assuming that he viewed me as a potential threat, I smiled, waved, and yelled, "It's okay!" Again, he didn't budge, but he did yell back, "I know it's okay because I ain't moving, mister."

Knowing that I had to do more to prove my intentions, I walked towards him, yelling over the speeding cars, "Dude! It's okay! I saw you biking along and figured that I'd offer you a ride."

"For real?????"

"For real," I said, extending my hand, "My name is David."

A huge smile broke out across his heavily bearded face, and he started talking. "Well, I am Bill, Bicycle-Bill…and I was just thinking about how I am gonna bake out here because it's so hot…"

He kept speaking while walking his bike towards my truck, but between the traffic noise and his bike's squeaking, I didn't hear much of what he was saying.

Bill began stripping his bike down to place it on my truck, but every few sentences he'd stop talking and say, "Are you for real?"

"Yes, I'm for real," I said

His skepticism continued as he stopped moving every few moments and said, "For real," and wait for me to reply. He asked if I was "for real" so often that I snapped, "Dude, this IS for real unless you keep asking, and then, I'm out."

"I'll shut up then," he said. But, he began talking moments later, "I just gotta say; I can't believe that this is for real."

I tried changing the topic by asking where he was going. "Waco," he said.

"I think that's on the way…I'll take you," I said.

"For real?"

"For real."

After getting his gear on board and settling down in my truck, I immediately realized the one drawback to picking up a homeless guy on the side of a hot highway.

Between his body odor and bad breath, Bill was pretty…ripe.

I quickly rolled the windows down as I accelerated onto I-35 towards Waco, and Bill stopped talking to ask, "Hey…doesn't the AC work in here??"

"It does…but we're gonna rock it like this, brother. Just sit back and chill."

Bill chilled for all of about 30 seconds and then sprang up to animatedly talk…a lot…about everything! As he spoke about everything, I could see beyond Bill's baggy clothes and take note of just how thin he was.

He chatted about being clean from drugs and alcohol, "Life is so much better now."

He talked about his faith and how reading the Bible calms him, "Sometimes I don't even read it and just sleep with it. It feels good to have it near."

He shared that he was lonely, "Since my friends got arrested, I'm by myself most of the time."

After speaking of his friend's arrest, he said, "Don't do a drug deal at a Walmart, Dave... you know why??...They have cameras EVERYWHERE. I knew this was a bad idea, and I told 'em not to go, and now they're gone."

He then mumbled something about "too many strikes" and became very melancholy and stared outside. Figuring that he talked himself to exhaustion, I just let Bill recline and enjoy the wind in his face. But then he popped right up and asked, "Dave, you single??"

"Yeah?" I said with great hesitancy.

Bill then put his hands behind his head and said, "Well, LOOK...AT...US, two good-lookin' single guys, cruising on the highway and living life: Ain't that America!!!" As he leaned back, with such a self-satisfied grin, it made me smile and give him a big high5.

The 80-mile drive to Waco went by quickly, and I was soon dropping Bicycle Bill off at a gas station off the highway.

After helping Bill with his gear, I leaned in to hug him, but he stopped me by saying, "I smell."

"No shit," I said.

We both laughed. Before I pulled off, Bill shared that sometimes people slow down to stare at him, some stop a "little ways" in front of him to leave a cold bottle of water or soda on the side of the road, and some even slow down to just yell at him.

"But," he paused, "no one has ever stopped to pick me up...except you, man."

We chatted a bit more, I hugged him and as I pulled off, he shouted: "You keep huggin' Dave; you make the world a better place to live...and I'm gonna pray for you, man!"

Thanks, Bill.

Gettin' Hugs at the Bunny Ranch

Carson City, Nevada. 2017

I was working at my job as a personal trainer when Dennis Hof's passing flashed across the news feed.

"Hey, I know that guy!" I shouted.

One person training dropped their weights and yelled, "What???" Then another person put their weights down and said, "Yeah, what??"

Soon, the whole gym was waiting for the story.

When driving throughout the nation on my Big Dave Hugs America, I was looking for crazy, off-beat places to hug people. Since I was already near Las Vegas, I thought, "The Bunny Ranch!!"

For those who don't know, The Bunny Ranch is a famous Nevada brothel owned by Dennis Hof, and assuming that it was near Las Vegas, I emailed them.

When I told one of my friends what I had done, they said, "Dave, you're crazy, and they'll think that you're a nut and never contact you."

Well, they did contact me, sort of.

What happened was that I received an email that said, " Is this legit?" with a signature that said "Dennis" with a cell number below it.

The problem was that "Dennis" accidentally CC'd me on this email, and I wasn't supposed to receive it.

Even though I wasn't supposed to be on this email thread, I couldn't help but reply with my two-cents regarding my legitimacy. So, I called Dennis' number.

The phone rang two times, and when a man answered, I asked if this was Dennis.

"Yeah??" the voice said.

"Well, man, I am very legit," is how I opened the call.

Knowing that he could hang up on me any moment, I treated the call as a sales call and immediately launched into what I hope to achieve on my tour. My sales skills must be sharp because Dennis ended up spending 15–20 minutes on the phone with me, and at one point, asked why I was doing this.

"Everyone needs to smile," I plainly said.

He laughed as he repeated my words, "everyone needs to smile."

Then, he said something like, "This guy IS the real deal" to someone else in the room who sounded like they also chuckled. Next, Dennis said, "I love this, but I hate to break it to you, man. We aren't in Vegas; we're in Carson City."

Because Carson City is about 7 hours north of Las Vegas, there was no way that I could make it there and stay on schedule.

Upon hearing this, Dennis sounded genuinely disappointed in this development and even asked what cities were on my itinerary to see if there was a way I could visit. When none of the towns on my route were close to his business, he told me to "be safe, What you're doing is good and know that you're always welcome at the Ranch" and then hung up.

The end...maybe.

Within minutes of our talk, I got a sizable anonymous donation sent to me with a note that said, "Keep going." I've no idea if the nameless donor was Dennis Hof—but it does make for a good story.

After sharing my story, one woman in the gym said, "David, ONLY YOU could have a feel-good story of a no-good pimp."

Moments vs. Monuments

Arizona. Colorado. New Mexico. Utah. 2017

I was probably ten years old when I first heard about the Four Corners Monument, the quadripoint where four states meet. Something about the description I read immediately conjured up these grand images of how cool it would be to travel there. But I was a kid, so any of my manifestations ended with, "One day when I'm older…"

So you can imagine my excitement when I was mapping out my 48 State Hugs & High5s Tour and pinpointing certain places that I just had to see. I thought back to those grand images I dreamt up so many years ago and thought, "One day…is TODAY."

I was in Durango, Colorado, the night before visiting the monument and woke up super early, like a kid at Christmas. Grinning the whole time, I sped through 100+ miles to reach the monument and have to say that it is a ridiculously simple one. It's just a super-sized, manhole-like medallion where Arizona, Colorado, New Mexico, and Utah meet. That's it.

I was a bit disappointed but waited in a long line to get to the "monument" with my "Big Dave Hugs America" sign anyway. As I stood in line, someone asked me what the story was with my sign.

As I spoke, I kept getting interrupted by people yelling, "Speak up," and "Louder." By the time I revealed this tour's purpose, someone yelled, "I want a hug," to which I had replied, "Okay."

But before I could step forward to hug that person, another voice yelled, "I want a high5."

"Who said that?" I said, looking at this long line of people. A woman standing directly in front of me looked around her and said with a shrug, "...all of us."

"Well, all right then," I said, and went hugging and high5-ing down the line. By the time I reached the end of the line, I had counted 72 hugs given. For the record, I kept a counter so I could keep an accurate record of my hugs.

A few more people wanted hugs, but I said that they would have to wait a minute because I didn't want to lose my spot in line.

"Don't worry, I got your spot, Big Dave," a voice yelled out. "Thanks," I shouted back.

When I made my way back up to the front of the line, here was an opportunity to live a moment that I'd dreamt about since I was a kid. But there was one drawback: I was alone and needed someone to take the picture for me. I asked the person behind me and he said, "Sure, but only if my kid can be in the picture with you. This is so cool—what you are doing."

I obliged, and in the picture above, you will see two kids—a real kid and me, a big kid.

Now, surrounding the monument are many kiosks where Native Americans sell a bunch of touristy knick-knacks and stuff, and as I was leaving, one of the vendors yelled out, "Big Dave, don't forget about us—we like hugs too."

"My bad," I said with a smile and walked over to hug them. When I reached them, one of the guys said, "Turn around."

"Why?"

"Just DO it," he said, putting his hand on my shoulder to spin me around.

When I turned around, the line of people I had just hugged and high5'd had morphed into one big mass of people who were now embracing, high5-ing and speaking with each other. As I watched this assemblage of humanity, I smiled, and the man with his hand on my shoulder pointed.

"I don't know who the hell you are," he said, "but that shit right there—is ALL YOU!!"

I hugged the guys and left thinking that the Four Corners Monument might have been underwhelming, but my four corners moment was everything I hoped it to be.

Just Two Guys on the Road

Somewhere in the USA

I was speeding along in one state.

No, wait a sec—I honestly thought that I was driving the speed limit in one state, but it was the police lights and siren that notified me that I might have been driving a bit too fast.

Because I believed I wasn't breaking any law, I rolled my window down with a smile and said, "Hey man, what's up, I was doing eighty."

"On the button," he said flatly, "but that's only the interstates' speed limit. The speed limit here is seventy."

"Oh, shit."

"Yup," he said.

As I fumbled for my license and registration, the state trooper took a step back from my car and asked what the "Big Dave Hugs America" magnetic placard was about.

Though he affirmatively nodded as I spoke about my travels worldwide and my current tour to hug all of America, his facial expression read as totally unimpressed. Before walking back to his car, he asked if I had any outstanding warrants or anything.

I smiled and told him I didn't but added, "I guess we'll find out together."

I sat on the windy, desolate highway for a long time—so long that I began to rethink my smart-ass comment to the trooper. I continued to rethink things even more, when I saw the officer begin to walk back to my car, holding a lot of papers.

Shit, I thought.

Once the officer was standing at my door, he held up the papers and my license and registration and said that I was driving through a great state.

"...and, one thing that this great state bequeaths to me is discretion," he continued.

He said that after hearing about what I was doing and looking me up in his vehicle, he believed me when I said that I thought that I was going the speed limit, so he wasn't giving me a speeding ticket.

"This isn't a citation. This here, is just a piece of paper saying that I radioed in, pulled you over, and am now talking to you—we are just two guys on the side of the road."

A bit puzzled by what was happening, I read over the document, signed it, and gave it back to the trooper, who said, "Good. Now that that is over, tell me what it's like."

"What?" I said.

"EVERYTHING!" he bellowed, extending his arms as if he were telling a big fish story.

"What's it like to want to be seen? What's it like to be loved by everyone, and give love? What's it like to do something this simple and this good? What's it like to be YOU?"

Here I thought that I was getting a ticket, and what I was getting was a great conversation instead.

With one eye on the dashboard clock—because I couldn't believe that we were having this talk—and my other eye on the officer, we spoke for almost 20 minutes about life.

At a pause in our chat, I asked, "Can I give you a hug?"

"What the hell do you think that I have been standing out here for? Hell yeah!" He said with a huge grin. Once out of the car, we hugged and talked some more. As he walked back to his car, I called back to him and said that I had something for him.

Duke Cannon, my tour sponsor, gave me some of their cooling Field Towels to give away to people. The Field Towels are a fantastic and refreshing way to cool off and freshen up if you are hiking, exercising, biking, or sitting in a squad car.

Yes, that was a blatant plug.

Anyway, I grabbed a few handfuls and said, "Hey, here ya go."

The officer looked at me and said he couldn't take it, because it could be interpreted as a bribe.

"Shit, if I thought that I could buy my way out of a ticket with a field towel, I would've been speeding all over this county. PLUS, you aren't a cop, remember? 'We are just two guys standing on the side of the road,' and you can accept any fucking thing I give you," I said.

"Damn, you caught that line."

"Yup."

Walking back to his car with a handful of Duke Cannon swag, the officer turned and said: "Hey Dave, let me ask you a question: if I had given you a ticket, would you have still given me this stuff?"

"Yeah, man, you doing your job isn't going to stop me from doing mine."

"Yeah, I figured as much. Keep being you, Dave."

Blindly Hugging

It isn't often that you meet someone who embodies your spirit, but I was fortunate to meet such a person in 2017.

I was in Houston on my Big Dave Hugs America Tour and had just introduced myself to a woman walking with a little blind girl. As I began describing my mission to embrace everyone I could, and what I hoped to accomplish by doing that, the little girl started smiling.

Her grin and energy grew with each detail I gave about my journey, and by the time her mother said, "Meet my daughter, Emily," the girl was clutching air in an attempt to get an embrace and asking, "Where is he? Where is he?"

Emily's enthusiasm was off the charts, and when I asked her mother to hug Emily, she replied, "How could I stop it?"

Kneeling to hug Emily was an experience. As soon as she felt my presence, she extended her arms to grab me tightly and said, "This is great!"

She didn't let me go for a few moments and just rocked back and forth with me. As much as I remember from Emily's hug, I also recall her mother's facial expression—so happy to see her daughter so elated. After a few moments, Emily let go of me with one hand and then began swatting at the air repeatedly, shouting, "Blind High5! Blind High5!"

I never heard that phrase before and watching her swinging and hitting nothing, I asked Emily for an explanation, "I just keep swiping 'til I hit something!"

I loved this answer because that is pretty much my attitude towards life.

Thank You, Emily; you're beautiful!

HELLO
my name is

Big Dave

#BigDaveHugsAmerica

The Happy Brother

Dallas, Texas. 2017

For my 48-state Hug and High5 Tour, I was extremely fortunate to partner with Advantage Rental Car. It has been a great relationship, and one of the unexpected benefits of our partnership was my having the opportunity to give motivational speeches to their staff every time I switched out cars.

When I switched out one car, there were maybe six or seven people working at that location, but that didn't stop me from speaking.

In actuality, I enjoy speaking to smaller groups because it gives me more latitude to change things up as a way to engage and potentially motivate people. My talk was going well, but as I was wrapping up, one more employee walked in.

Feeling the vibe that I was putting out there, she rolled her eyes and openly groaned, "Oh Lord. The 'Happy Brotha' is here."

Her statement seemed to delight the others, and since I've heard this before and didn't want to waste anyone's time, I stopped talking for a moment. After a short pause, I said, "Indulge me for just one more minute.

"Check it," I continued. "If I told you that the owner of this company asked someone, 'Can you make America happy?' and the person who said 'yes' and shook their hand was about to walk through that door right there, right now—would you think that person would look, act or sound ANYTHING like my old, black, foul-mouthed ass?"

Silence.

Then, one employee looked at the doorway and back at me and said, "Oh shit, he's right."

Jumping on that affirmative moment, I said, "That's right! The very fact that I am here means that your dream, your desire, your passion, possibility, your desire, and your wants are ALL possible,"—making sure to point directly at someone's chest each time I said the word "your."

I went on to say that dream fulfillment isn't easy. "You have to point the finger at yourself and have all I's dotted, T's crossed, budgets written and all that shit—just wanting something isn't nearly enough—you have to put that work in."

Someone else groaned, and while I didn't know why they did so, I elected to go on the offensive.

"Let me ask you: if you were living the dream, YOUR dream, and knew that all of your other dreams were possible—not real, not easy, just possible—how could you not smile every day? Why would you not help others, if for nothing else, so they don't grow up to be disgruntled 'haters' and eventually try and stop or rob your ass?! How could you stop yourself from offering someone a hug, knowing that they may succeed in an area where you don't and possibly help you down the line? If that is how you saw life—and THAT IS HOW I SEE LIFE —how could I not smile? How could I not be the happy brother? Oh yeah, I heard you," I said with a wink to the person who'd initially moaned.

"How could I not be me?" Again, silence.

Then one woman who was eating lunch in the break room stood up, wiped a tear from her eye, and proclaimed, "This was the best lunchtime talk ever, come here and give me a hug before I have to go back to work."

If You're Lucky Enough

Dodge City, Kansas. 2017

When I was coming up with my Hugs and High5s itinerary, visiting Dodge City wasn't anywhere on my list.

But as I sat in a Wichita, Kansas café where everyone I encountered was extremely—how do I say this?—less than enthusiastic about getting a hug, high5 or even a smile from me, I made a change.

Let me stop you before you think that some considerable amount of thought went into this decision; there wasn't, I simply saw a 'Visit Dodge City' billboard on my way out of Wichita and began driving.

I am so glad for that billboard because I might have missed meeting one very cool man. The cool guy I am speaking of is Bill, a 97-year-old Dodge City resident.

Bill and I met in the Dodge City Saloon, a part of The Boot Hill Museum, where you virtually step back in time to stroll the streets as they were in the 1800's. The museum is pretty cool and offers you the opportunity to watch staged gunfights and meet actors portraying the men and women who tamed the old west.

Through a conversation about our lives and travels, Bill revealed that he was a part of WWII's D-Day invasion of Normandy on Day One.

But hours before the storming the beach, he was pulled out of his rank and file by his supervising officer and told he was being held back for the battle's second day.

Bill said he gave little thought to the decision and assumed he would find out why he was pulled from his unit later on.

But, he never discovered why because within hours of that decision, all of his comrades and their commanding officer were dead.

"All I know is that I am alive because of that decision," he calmly said.

Living without an explanation for this life-saving decision gave him a great deal of survivor's guilt and grief. Tormented by life's turn of events, Bill said he "was forced to figure things out."

After some hard years, he concluded that life boils down to one simple thing: If you are lucky enough to get another day, use it.

He said this outlook simplified his life.

This new perspective brought him peace as well as an ability to find a way through problems that would have previously stopped him in life. It was a great conversation that I wanted to continue, but Bill said he was tired and he thought he already "gave me enough."

"I believe you got what you came for. Now go and hug some people, but take it easy on 'em—you're a strong man."

We hugged and as we did, I said the first words of his credo and he reciprocated by saying them softly back to me:

"If you're lucky enough."

Now Serving Hugs

Twin Falls, Idaho. 2017

Whenever I see a Chick-fil-A, I recall the time—possibly the only time—that they stopped serving chicken sandwiches for hugs.

I was in Idaho near the Snake River Canyon and while waiting at the drive-thru window, the cashier asked what the 'Big Dave Hugs America' magnetic sign on my car was all about. As I began to share the mission behind the car sign and my backstory, the cashier's eyes widened with amazement.

Next, a flurry of rapid-fire questions came my way. "What's the best place you've visited?"

"Where are people the nicest?"

"Do you get scared?"

"Do you get tired?"

"Do you get lonely?"

I patiently answered all of her questions, but when my food was finally ready and bagged up, she held it back for one more question.

"Do people treat you kindly all over the world?"

After answering, I saw what I believed to be an authentic look of disappointment because I was leaving her face and said. "Would it be cool if I came in and gave you a hug?"

"Oh my God," she cooed, "…that would be so cool!"

As I drove away, I could hear her yell, "He's coming in y'all!!"

When I entered the eatery, the manager was waiting for me at the counter, like a head of state, with a bunch of the staff standing behind him.

Smiling, he extended his hand to shake and much to the delight of the cashier who was standing right beside him, I asked if he wanted a hug or high5 instead.

He obliged me on both and asked if I could repeat my story.

I began to speak but was interrupted mid-sentence by the manager who yelled to his back house staff who were craning their necks to hear/see what was going on. "Guys c'mon up here: this story is amazing and good…Sorry, sir, can you start over."

I began speaking again until the girl taking the drive-thru orders began grousing about no one else was working. Then it happened. The manager said, "Hold 'em up for a minute and tell them that we're on a hug break."

The next thing I heard was, "Umm..thanks for coming to Chick-fil-A we are takin' a…hug…break for a minute. Please bear with us."

It sounded so cool to me, but the manager's facial expression said, "that ain't right" and ran over to smooth things over with the customers.

Seeing that I was creating chaos, I ate my food in the dining room, and the staff came over one-by-one for hugs and high5s.

The Strong and Silent Type

Billings Montana. 2017

On my Big Dave Hugs America Tour, I did what you are not supposed to do; I picked up a hitchhiker. I KNOW that I shouldn't, but I did.

Well, he wasn't actually hitchhiking.

I was driving on a desolate stretch of highway a few hours outside of Billings, Montana and saw this old guy sitting on the roadside. I pulled over to see if he was okay and once he said he was, I told him to get in and I would drive him to his destination.

Once in the car, he introduced himself as Jerry and said that he was tired and resting from lugging a deer carcass onto his property. He noted that the carcass was big enough to feed his six dogs for a long time and didn't say much afterward.

For most of the 15-mile drive to his home, Jerry remained silent unless I asked him something. It wasn't until I drove on the road to his property that he said anything, really.

That's when he moved his hands like someone was talking and dryly said, "You know, you talk a lot."

His words made us both laugh as well and made for a great picture.

Thanks, Jerry.

That's Not A Gun
In My Pants.

Canyonville, Oregon. 2017

A natural byproduct of taking risks in life and winning is that you become even bolder with the next set of risks that you take.

You can't control it. Moreover, you don't even realize it. You are just doing what you do.

And, before you know it, you are just taking bigger and bigger chances. It just happens.

I was getting bolder, some would say "riskier" while on my Big Dave Hugs America Tour.

At the outset of the tour, I was my usual extroverted self, but I was even more daring by the time I had driven throughout half the country and hugged a few thousand people. I was going out of my way and approaching people I didn't believe I had a chance to hug, high5, or even engage with.

Nothing is more demonstrative of this than when I drove through a parking lot and jumped out of my car to ask a bunch of leather-clad, beer-drinking guys leaning on their motorcycles for a hug.

Our contrasting styles were stark; they wore boots, jeans, and leather jackets with their motorcycle club's name stitched in, and I wore cargo shorts, a polo shirt, some Air-Jesus sandals, and a smile. Clearly, I was an outsider, but that didn't stop me from asking for an embrace.

Standing amid a group of guys, I heard, "What tha fuck did you say you wanted?"

"A hug."

"What??"

"A hug."

I was nervous but stood my ground and said that I didn't mean any disrespect and quickly explained what I was doing. Afterward, I then put up my hand and said:"...or I could get a high5."

The men just looked at me perplexed and said, "get tha hell out of here..go talk to the president with that bullshit."

"Cool," I said and approached who I presumed was in charge. When I did, the conversation was pretty much the same.

"What?" he said.

"...a hug," I repeated.

"What?' he repeated.

"A hug or a high5," I countered as if bargaining at a bazaar.

"Get da fuck out of here...for real??" he said.

Now drawing a bit of a crowd, I flatly said, "No bullshit," and told my story again.

"For real...you are out here hugging white folks...ALONE??"

"Yeah!"

"Why"

"Because someone has to," I said.

"Why you?"

"Because someone has to," I repeated.

"Get the fuck outta here—who's in his truck?" he said, nodding to his people who were now glancing through my truck's open passenger side window.

One of them shouted, "No one!...he's alone."

"Get the fuck out of here! You're hugging white folks alllllllllll across America by yourself," he exclaimed with disbelief and followed up with, "...are you packing?"

I knew that he was referencing a gun, but I don't carry, so I grabbed my crotch and replied with, "...just this dick."

One of the members standing by him did a literal spit take with his beer as everyone else began chuckling.

Not laughing at all and speaking with what sounded like a hint of concern, the president asked if I at least had a knife.

"Yeah, but it's in my luggage and it would take me 20 minutes to find it, so I just have to talk my way into or out of something like I am hopefully doing right now," I said.

There was a pause, and the president said, "Wow! Yo, give this big mother-fucker a hug."

The Horse Stays
In The Picture

Minnesota. 2017

Shortly after entering Minnesota on my Big Dave Hugs America Tour, I passed an Amish farmer driving a horse-drawn cart.

Thinking that it would be a fun picture to have, almost like a modernized twist of Grant Wood's *American Gothic,* I pulled over and asked to take a picture.

The farmer's name was Dan, and he wasn't nearly as enthusiastic about taking a picture as I was.

Let me see if I can recall precisely what he said when I asked to take his picture …Oh yeah, I believe that was, "NO!"

But after speaking to me for a little while, he did soften his stance a bit and said, "Look, I'll hold your sign if it will help bring about some peace in this world—and you can get a picture of Scotty," his horse.

Dan and I never hugged or high5'd, but I did get a friendly nod and smile that displayed there is always a way to connect.

The Hug I Didn't Give

Chicago, Illinois. 2017

Ten thousand hugs was the goal when planning my Big Dave Hugs America Tour.

Embracing that many people throughout 48 states in 77 days was a lofty goal, but I believed it could be done.

Every day on that tour, I woke up with only one thing on my to-do list: to positively engage with as many people as possible and hope that they accepted an embrace.

With my doing all of the driving, planning, hugging, and high5-ing, the tour wasn't always easy. But, I was doing a pretty good job throughout the nation and kept a counter with me to accurately record my hug-tally.

By the time I reached Chicago, Illinois, there were still over three weeks remaining in my tour, and I woke up feeling excited because my hug count was at 9,998 people.

I joked with one of my friends that I could reach my goal by hugging the hotel maids and didn't even have to leave my hotel room. Of course that wasn't the case, though. I had a packed schedule of offering hugs and high5s throughout the Windy City all day.

But I needed coffee first.

I strolled into a cafe as soon as it opened and was the third person in line. "Any one of these customers or baristas could be my 10,000th hug," I happily thought. Just as I reached the register, one of the three baristas working went to the back storeroom to answer a phone call. Within moments, a shriek filled the café.

"Oh my God, no! Not Momma!!"

After hearing that, all you heard was loud sobbing.

The whole café stopped in its tracks for a long uncomfortable moment until one barista ran to the back to see what was wrong. The customers stood there, not saying a word until the lone barista working finished preparing the two drinks ordered before me and awkwardly said, "Can I take the next guest's order, please?"

"Double espresso over ice," I said, quickly followed by, "Uhh…is she going to be alright?"

"I don't know…let me get on that drink for you."

By the time my drink was brewed, one barista had emerged from the backroom and somewhat whispered that the other barista's mother had suddenly passed away.

"Oh shit," a customer said.

As soon as I heard this, I informed the baristas about what I'd been doing all summer and said I was more than willing to hug this woman.

"It sounds like she REALLY needs it," I said.

"I will tell her," said the barista.

I sat at a table closest to the storeroom and waited for almost 20 minutes to hug this woman, but she never came through the door.

"I don't think she's coming out, man, sorry," one barista said. I could still hear her weeping when I left.

The person pictured is the 10,000th person I embraced.

Manifest Destiny

Detroit, Michigan. 2017

I met a chess-hustling homeless guy in a Detroit park who obliged me for a hug and a high5 but seemed puzzled by my tour's mission and who I was.

"Are you military?…A cop?…A fireman?…Rich?…Religious?…Retired?" he asked.

When my reply to all of his queries was "no," and I went into more detail about my life and travels, he said, "So you are just a nice guy—SHIT, I didn't know that they even still made you motherfuckers."

That was when his friend piped up from a nearby chess table.

"So let me get this straight—how long have you been hugging folks?"

"My whole life, I guess. But, as a mission: for the last sixteen years or so since 2001."

"Yo, man," he said to the first homeless man, "he's more than a nice guy. He created his own job, his own reality. Shit, he breathed life into his own existence. Yo, he's the fuckin' man!"

That was when the first guy spoke again: "Yo, man, that sign should read: Hello, my name is Big Dave, a nice guy."

"Next time," I said. ˙

I asked if I could take his picture. He said that it was gonna be a "few dollars," and when I asked if we could play chess, he said that it would cost me a "few dollars more" if I lost to him.

I took the first option and paid him for a picture. Go out and create your own reality, people, you won't be disappointed.

Mahalo

Rochester, New York. 2017

I made a bit of a last-minute addition to my Big Dave Hugs America Tour and stopped in Rochester on my way through New York State.

The Parkleigh Stationery Store were big supporters of my sponsor, Duke Cannon Soap, as well as my hug mission and showed their enthusiasm as soon as I entered.

The manager hugged me right away, and excitedly said, "You have to hug our customers." With that, she handed me the phone for the store's intercom and said, "Tell your story."

"Good afternoon, shoppers…" is how I began sharing my story with the customers. It felt cool to be a sort of "motivational DJ" for the store. But, within moments of finishing, a woman excitedly stood in front of me and practically screamed, "Me first! Me first! I just got off a plane from Hawaii and love hugs and really need one."

Standing behind this woman was her friend who just affirmatively shook her head like a great hype-man and said, "Yeah, she needs a hug."

I was going to hug her anyway, but her excitement and hype-man prompted

267

me to ask, "Why?" She explained that she just got off of a plane from Hawaii because she was bringing her recently deceased husband home.

Reading my puzzled expression correctly, she opened up her leather bag hanging off her shoulder just enough to let me see a package that I assumed contained her husband's ashes. As she gently patted the package, she said, "Sooooooo…I love hugs, need one, and my husband was a big guy like you. Can you hug me like he did?"

It was an odd request for sure, but after listening to her story, all I could say was, "Uhh…I'll try—what was his name?"

"Whitey," she said dryly.

We both laughed and, lifting my hand as if I were raising a glass in a toast, I said, "For Whitey" and gave her a long hug.

As we embraced, I could feel her body shudder a bit as she began to cry and felt her tears dampen the side of my face. As they did, she whispered "Mahalo"—the Hawaiian word for "thank you"—in my ear and continued holding me for a while.

By the time we finished embracing, everyone around us was shedding a collective tear.

Watch out for Whitey—he'll get ya crying every time.

Semper Fi

Westborough, Massachusetts. 2017

Meet Sergeant William Carr.

We met while I was driving through Westborough, Massachusetts. I wish there was some grand narrative about our encounter, but there isn't.

The truth is, I just saw the 88-year-old man walking down a street by himself in his full-dress Marine uniform and thought, "He looks cool; I wonder if he wants a hug."

That fleeting thought was all it took for me to impulsively pull my car over, jump out and say, "Thank you for your service" and offer him a hug.

He didn't say anything for a few moments, and then said, "I guess that you're alright." He stepped toward me, but at the last second, he stopped and said, "Wait, are they free?"

"For you? Sure," I said with a smile and smart-ass snicker.

After our hug, we chatted and I asked if he needed a ride. This time, it was his turn to have a smart-ass comment, and he stepped back to examine me from head to toe and said, "I guess you're okay."

I drove him to a nearby cafe, where he said they fed him for free and said, "Here you are!"

But he had other plans.

He looked over at me, rolled his eyes, and said, "I'm not getting out... We're TALKIN'!"

I put the car in park and then listened to stories from his varied life—from his dad being a stunt flyer and knowing how to fly before he could drive, to his combat stints in World War II and Korea, to working on Apollo 11 and more.

He was a fascinating man.

When he finished speaking, he gathered himself to get out of the car and said, "Semper Fi," the US Marine Corps' motto, to which I said, "I am not a Marine."

Already halfway out of the car, he steadied himself with his cane to get back in the car and stiffly turned his body to pat me on the chest above my heart. "No, you aren't," he said, "but you are a warrior doing good things, and that's enough. Semper Fi."

Semper Fi, Sergeant.

It Takes One
to Know One

Nantucket, Massachusetts. 2017

It isn't every day that you meet someone who has survived a shark attack, but on one September day in Nantucket, I did.

Paul de Gelder is a former Australian underwater demolitions expert; how bad-ass do you have to be to qualify for that job?! He was on a training exercise off the Sydney, Australia coast when a bull shark attacked him. Because I don't believe that any of my words could do his incredible story justice, I will give you the most basic details.

Once attacked, Paul had to keep his wits about himself enough to swim through his own blood to a nearby boat's safety where his mates had to pinch off an artery to save his life.

And, that's just the beginning of his story.

As I sat and listened to his full story, each intense detail drew me in.

I couldn't help but mutter the word "bad-ass" repeatedly, as he vividly described what it felt like to lose his leg and arm and then go through his long road through recovery. In listening to him curse with every other word and continuously speak about moving forward in life, I felt like I had a kindred spirit in Paul.

When he asked about my life and travels and kept calling *me* a "bad-ass," I chalked it off to his being extremely polite. Even if he was full of shit, being called a "bad-ass" by him was an honor, I thought.

After speaking for a while, I hugged Paul good-bye and walked away, believing that our paths would never cross again. But as it turned out, Paul was on the same air-shuttle that I was on.

Because I was the last man to board this small plane, I stood at the doorway and announced that I was offering high5s to anyone who wanted one.

Yes, I am THAT guy.

As I walked down the narrow airplane aisle, smiles beamed up to greet me, and hands were raised to meet mine. By the time I reached Paul's seat, his prosthetic arm was raised, and he was shaking his head with a massive grin on his face.

After we high5'd, Paul laughingly said, "Who else does this shit—except for a Badass?!"

It takes one to know one. Thank you, Paul.

Please do yourself a favor—Google his story and get ready to be inspired.

It's Too Late

San Antonio, Texas. 2017

After the mass shooting at the First Baptist Church in Sutherland Springs, Texas, I went down to offer hugs to people in the Parrish for the Christmas holidays. To get there, I had to fly into San Antonio, where I was greeted happily by an elderly couple, Harriet and Papa Joe.

The tiny retired couple had a kiosk in the airport lobby where they would direct people to rental cars, ground transport, and field other frequently asked questions.

After answering my question about where to find the rental car desk, Harriet asked why I was visiting San Antonio. After explaining my purpose for visiting, she said, "Hugs for the holiday, that really is beautiful.... Now, go away before you start making me cry."

"OK," I said and began to turn away.

I never entirely made a full turn away from Harriet, though, because she suddenly yelled, "It's too late!!!...come here, bend down and hug me." She then hugged me and cried on my shoulder.

Now, Papa Joe had been doing something else this whole time and didn't pay us too much attention until he saw Harriet crying. When he asked what was going on, Harriet said, "…just give the man a hug, and I'll explain later. He has to go."

"Oh OK," he said as he came over to me, and then the three of us shared an embrace.

Welcome

Mount Rushmore, South Dakota.

Under the unflinching granite eyes of George Washington, Abraham Lincoln, Thomas Jefferson, and Theodore Roosevelt at the Mount Rushmore Monument in South Dakota, I had the honor of meeting and hugging the Charles family of northern Virginia.

What made this family stand out among many of the others I've met on my travels was that they were a black family on their way to visiting all 50 states.

The patriarch of the family, his name escapes me, shared with me that he had traveled a lot as a young man and expressed how it impacted his future. It was great comparing travelogues with him because, between the two of us, we had covered much of the world and been significantly inspired by it. He said that he wanted that same impact for his children and promised them that they would visit every state before college.

"Travel just makes you dream bigger, man," he said.

As we were getting ready to take this picture, his niece—who I am hugging—said, "Oh my God, what he's doing is so cool...why can't we take a cool trip like he's doing"

"Because this man is on a mission...AND he has a sponsor," he quipped.

It was a great moment to capture, and I never thought I would hear from this family again.

But I did.

Over a year later and within minutes of formally announcing that I was staging a two-week, seven-city hug tour through Alaska, I got a great message:

> *Welcome to the 50 State Club, we've been waiting for you.*
> THE CHARLES FAMILY.

Giving Hope
and Happiness

Kenai Alaska. 2018

When visiting Kenai, Alaska, I arranged to speak to a small group of high school students touring Kenai Peninsula College from Utqiagvik, Alaska—formally Barrow.

Utqiagvik is a small town at the top of Alaska and one of the planet's northernmost cities.

When speaking, I believed that I wasn't connecting with the students because they pretty much sat stone-faced through my picture-punctuated talk.

Usually, I get a lot of feedback on my talks, but I wrapped things up pretty quickly since the kids were silent.

Later that evening, I happened upon one of the teen group's chaperones, who said the kids loved my talk and couldn't stop talking about it.

"That's news to me; they didn't say anything."

She explained that kids are taught not to question adults in their culture, but they paid close attention and were more than impressed.

"You know you're giving away a lot more than hugs, right?"

"Yeah, I'm giving high5s, too," I quipped.

Pursing her lips and shaking her head in an admonishing way as if to say, 'get serious, kid,' she said, "You don't get it, do you?! You are giving people hope. You are a man of color...who is happy and so happy that he's just giving happiness away. I've never seen anything like you, and I know the kids haven't either."

You ever have one of those times when someone gives you a new perspective on something you thought you knew everything about? Yeah, well, this was my time.

Her words shook me to seriousness, and I sat down on a chair next to her. Now staring up at her, I continued to listen.

"Do not stop doing what you are doing, not for a moment." She paused to hug me and afterward said, "and stay happy; the world needs you," with a big smile.

A Man Going Somewhere

Anchorage, Alaska. 2018

On my first full day in Alaska, I was standing in a line at a popular Anchorage cafe in a bit of a jet-lagged fog when the man standing behind me said, "Excuse me, but you look like a man that is going somewhere in life...I just get a...'feeling' about it."

Thinking that he was referencing my "Big Dave Hugs the World" sign that I usually carry with me when I am on hug trips, I said, "Did the sign give it away?"

"What sign...?" he asked.

Looking down and realizing that I left my sign in my rental car, I said, "Holy shit...Yeah, I kind of am going somewhere."

Because I am always eager to meet new people, I offered to share a table with the man and his son, who was standing with him in line so we could continue chatting.

279

Once seated, Wille Templeton introduced me to his son, Joseph, who has Down's Syndrome. "Joseph," he said, "this is Big Dave, and he's been going somewhere for a long time now. Will you sit quietly, please?"

Joseph complied, and Willie shared his fascinating life story of contracting a flesh-eating virus that nearly took his leg along with his life. He said that while quarantined in the hospital, he had an epiphany: "It occurred to me that I hadn't seen much of the world and Joseph had seen less, and if I die, he will see none of it."

With that revelation in his mind, he said that he prayed for his own recovery and described how he slowly pulled through. He said that his first fully healthy act was to retire and speak to a travel agent.

"From that point on," Willie said with a smile, "Joseph and I have been out seeing the world!" Willie even had a book about Hawaii with him because he and Joseph had a trip coming up.

It was a great honor to hug these two guys who were also going somewhere in life.

Finding an Angel
on Craigslist

Virginia Beach, Virginia. 2019

Let me preface this story by saying that I entered into my book's writing/self-publishing process knowing nothing.

I knew less than nothing if you need me to be more specific.

Like most of my life travels, I trusted my instincts for this process and chose those paths that felt best. That's my roundabout way of saying I got really lucky here.

Now to the story.

When I finished the first draft of *Traveling at the Speed of Life* in 2009, I felt the stories were good, but they were raw, rife with typos, run-on sentences, fragments, spelling errors, and some rambling consciousness streams. In short, the book needed work, but without much of a budget, my options were severely limited.

So, I went to where all the great writers go: Craigslist!

I can't recall my post's exact wording, but it said something like: I am a first-time author looking for an editor of a book of my travels around the world that will hopefully motivate others to see more and be more.

Most of the responses for editorial services weren't legitimate, and some were even solicitations for sex. But, of all the responses, there was one that stood apart from them all.

Enter Malini, one of my post's first responders, who stated that she was looking for an inspiring side project to channel her energies.

As I read her email, I couldn't believe my good fortune. "She's perfect," I thought. When we met a week later, I really couldn't believe my good luck. Arriving early for our meeting with a big smile, a resumé and a long list of books that she had read, she was even more impressive than anticipated.

The more she spoke, the more my instincts screamed, "don't mess this up," and I found myself working hard to dazzle her.

By the end of our coffee meeting, we agreed that she would read through a couple of my strongest chapters and then give me her opinion on working with me. "Well, alright!!! Let's seal this deal with a hug!!" I shouted. As she walked away, I found myself feeling like I had been on a date rather than a screening process. All I could think was, "I hope she works with me."

I didn't have to wait long for an answer.

After reading my chapters, Malini said that she was willing to work with me to help focus my writing so the stories didn't meander, but that I would have to get a professional editor to fix the many grammatical errors.

The "heart and soul of a great book" is present, she wrote.

She ended her email with, "...if your writing can keep me inspired, you have my services for free until you publish."

This news was better than excellent; it was beautiful.

We got to work right away with a simple schedule: every week, Malani would receive a couple of chapters then give me her edits within a few days. Once received, we'd go over them on the phone, and then I'd get to work on the rewrites.

I didn't know if this was the process that other writers-editors-publishers employed, but my instincts were guiding me, and this felt right, so I stuck with it.

As our system repeated itself over the next few months, Malini's influence and insight became invaluable. As the book quickly shaped up, she suggested that I drop some chapters because they just didn't "fit" anymore. You know what? She was right, and I did just that.

When we completed the editing process, it was just at the right time for both of us. Malini needed to focus on moving her family away from Philadelphia, and I had to begin concentrating on other aspects of the book, like the cover art, formatting, font size, the trim, and other steps in the self-publishing process.

At the time of *Traveling at the Speed of Life*'s publication, Malini had moved to Washington DC, and we only saw each other in social media posts… until seven years later in Virginia Beach.

I was staging a hug-party in a cafe after a mass shooting left 12 people dead and the community reeling. As I was waiting to hug some people, I heard, "David??…is that you??"

With a smile as radiant as sunshine, Malini was standing before me, and I couldn't believe it.

"What are you doing here??" I asked.

She explained that she was driving home from vacationing in the Carolinas and decided to stop in Virginia Beach.

"I just came in here because it looked cool," she said. What are the odds— I can't make this up.

All that said, meet Malini—a brilliant woman, super mom, a beautiful wife, and a guiding angel for my book. She is the person with the best hug story for this book but not the only person to help *Traveling at the Speed of Life* get into shape.

I dedicate this chapter to those game-changing souls: Anne, Ben Denise, Ellen, Eric, Jason, Jim, Leigh, Malini, Mary, and Maurice.

I couldn't have done it without you.

Twice

Virginia Beach, Virginia. 2019

Malini wasn't the only person at the Green Cat Juice Bar who I embraced before.

The other person was a woman who worked in the same building where the May 31st municipal building mass shooting occurred but was on another floor.

She stopped by the cafe for a hug and then looked at me through extremely puffy eyes that barely held back tears and detailed what happened on the day of the shooting. She spoke about hearing shots and began to talk about what she did afterward but stopped talking when other people stopped by for an embrace.

Sniffling and furiously wiping away tears to appear calm, she said, " I don't know how much I can take..I am just going to leave."

I looked at her with her lip quivering and suggested that she sit and stay a while. "You can help me hug people," I said.

After being my embracing-sidekick for a few people, this woman quietly sat down and began looking at a running slide show of hug pictures I had set up on my laptop.

Suddenly, she exclaimed, "Wait!! I think that I hugged you before…Were you at Virginia Tech?"

"Yup, "I said.

"Oh my god! Oh my god—this can't be I was a freshman there during that shooting too!! NOW you understand - I really can't take any more of this!!" she said, sobbing.

The realization that we hugged at two mass shooting locations was a very sobering and somber revelation and had me wondering, "how much can any of us take?"

The wounds of mass shootings and violence go much deeper than a bullet. Family, friends, and community members continue to bear the emotional trauma of these acts of terror long after the news of the story fades.

I am just a dude who likes hugging people and NOT A MENTAL HEALTH PROFESSIONAL—so consider the source of these suggestions.

If you know of someone who's experienced some emotional trauma, here are a few things you can do

Text them to say, "Hi."

Be patient.

Reach out to them to ask how they are and then listen to them. Hug them until they hug you back.

Do what you can to connect and do it now because we've all been through a lot, and I don't know how much more any of us can take.

Thank you, Jeanie Landis and the Green Cat Cafe ownership and staff—your cafe is magical.

I Remember

Belle Fourche, South Dakota. 2019

My 2018 Valentine's Day Hug Party at the geographic center, or heart, of the contiguous United States in Lebanon, Kansas, was so fulfilling that I staged another party for the following year.

The 2019 version was at the heart of the nation, given Alaska and Hawaii, in Belle Fouche, South Dakota.

Initially, I planned to keep my hug party confined to a local community center for seniors, but the center's executive director Laura Bennet had other plans. My story so touched her that she took the liberty of planning a 12-hour hug itinerary for me.

I got a good night's sleep after I arrived in Belle Fourche and am glad I did because I needed all of my energy for the hug-day ahead.

My Valentine's Day began at 7:45 AM when I addressed a packed assembly at the local high school. The response was remarkably enthusiastic, which invigorated me for my next stops at department stores, a hunting shop, a yoga studio, the library, a museum, the police station, and a few other places.

Late in the afternoon, I visited a healthcare facility for the elderly and, I have to tell you, I love visiting these places. At senior centers, you can always count on hearing a few good stories and fascinating accounts and perspectives on significant historical events.

And, no one is more appreciative of your time and presence than a senior citizen. Go volunteer at your local senior center and see it all for yourself; it's incredible.

Everyone at the facility from the residents down to the custodians had an enormous amount of Valentine's Day spirit and wanted a hug and high5. I even got a few kisses on the cheek from a few residents. The energy in the memory unit, where most of the residents have Alzheimer's, was a bit more subdued, though. Most of the individuals there were content to keep to themselves.

One patient, though, was bright-eyed and waiting in a common area. She called me over to the sofa where she was seated by waving to me with a smile. When I stood before her, she motioned with her finger to come even closer, and when I bent down to her level, she sat up straight and hugged me around the neck. After letting me go, she looked at me and said, "I am not in my right mind, I know that. But I am clear now and think that what you are doing is beautiful. Please keep going."

I thought that it was such a sweet and honest thing to say and began to sit down to continue speaking with her, but she pushed against me on my hip. "No! Go do your job; hug. Hug!!"

As I walked away to continue doing 'my job,' I did it with a massive smile on my face and looked forward to having another moment with this nice lady, but there wasn't going to be another moment.

As I returned to the common area, I could see that a vacant stare had replaced the spark of vitality in the woman's eye. My grin faded as I realized that our moment was gone, and I walked away to continue to 'go do my job' with a tear in my eye.

I can't forget that.

Big Mike

Fox Chase Cancer Center.

In December 2018, my friend Evelyn said that her friend, Mary, "needed" my hugs and energy because she was suffering under the strain of dealing with multiple myeloma, a blood cancer.

Unaware of my ability to really do anything, I did what I could by delivering a picture punctuated talk of my hug travels. Using only my happiest photographs and sharing the most uplifting stories, my informal speech had the three of us crying, laughing, and hugging each other.

Afterward, we went to lunch, and it was a continuous emotional mixture of heartfelt stories, tears, laughs, and more hugs. I would like to believe that I helped sustain enough good vibes to help Mary fight through the infusions, treatments, and chemo.

On April 26, 2019, Mary went through her last round of chemotherapy and after years of treatment, she finally got the chance to ring the Fox Chase Cancer Center Survivor's Bell.

To mark this special occasion, Evelyn arranged for Mary's family to be waiting for her with flowers, cake, and balloons when she exited into the waiting area.

Mary was so surprised to see her friends and everything else that she immediately burst into tears.

As she hugged and thanked everyone, Mary smiled and yelled, "Oh, my god, Big Mike!! Y-y-you're!" Chemo-brain can make your head a bit fuzzy.

"Yeah, I am," I said with a smile and a big embrace.

The emotion of the moment made me think of my father's ordeal with cancer. It also prompted me to walk around the lobby area to offer hugs and cake to the other patients and supporters.

A patient named Wendy embraced me and said, "Thank you, I wanna ring the hell out of that bell one day."

"You will, Wendy, you will," I said.

Another patient needed help up from his wheelchair to hug me and said, "It's a shame that my wife isn't here to get a hug. But, that's OK; I'll take hers." After we hugged for a while, he plopped down in his chair and jokingly said, "You're really good at this. You should do this for a living."

"I kinda do," I said.

"Well, then you are livin' the life, Big Mike, I mean livin' the life," he said with a huge smile.

Talk to Strangers

The Union League of Philadelphia.

As a child, I was told not to talk to strangers but never listened; I took things in the complete opposite direction and spoke to everyone. Then, as an adult, I offered hugs to strangers, and this image pretty much captures all of that.

While in a cafe one morning, I noticed a family looking down at a map and debating which way to go. Because I have been in that position many times on my travels, I spoke up and asked, "Where y'all trying to go?" As soon as they began speaking, I noticed their thick Australian accent and asked where they lived.

"Perth," one of them said.

"I have a friend in Perth," I said with a smile and immediately began chatting about what they were doing in Philadelphia.

They said that they had just driven down from NYC, on their way to Washington DC, and were making a quick stop to take a picture at the "Rocky" statue.

"That changes NOW," I declared as a proud Philadelphian.

I quickly began selling them on the sights, history, and food that my city had to offer—including the Liberty Bell, Fairmount Park, the Reading Terminal Market, the Art Museum steps that Rocky famously climbed, and everything in between.

I was selling the city hard, but my biggest play was to offer them a personalized tour of The Union League of Philadelphia.

Founded in 1862, The Union League of Philadelphia is the nation's oldest and one of the most respected private clubs. The historic building is one square block and houses a museum, event spaces, three restaurants, a library, a hotel, and a health club. But the best part about the Union League is that I am employed there, so my offer of a tour was an easy one.

After the tour, they wanted a picture outside, and as we posed, a woman abruptly stopped walking in front of us so as not to ruin our image.

"C'mon, get in this picture," I said with a smile.

The young woman hesitated for a moment but then smiled and said, "OK," and posed with us.

After the picture, the young woman said that she was having a bit of a bad morning and that it was so bad that she decided to stop by a bakery and get a cupcake with her name on it for breakfast. "Cupcakes always make me smile," she stated with a smile.

"But," she added "This is good too," pointing to all of us and smiling. "It's gonna be a good day," I said, giving her a high5.

"It seems like it," she said, still grinning.

I realize that many people are afraid to take the time to speak with people who they don't know. But, I am here to tell you that I have been doing it my whole life and have had more happy moments like these around the world than bad ones.

That said, meet The Tucker's of Perth, Australia: Celeste, Daniel, and Laurence. And, meet Mia…at least, that's what I think her name is. She had taken a bite out of the cupcake, and all I could see was "M-I-A."

A Big Knight

Bromley, UK. 2019

I was supposed to stay in a hotel in the heart of London while on my Big Dave Hugs & High5s Europe and Israel Tour. But, due to Hotwire issues that still have me heated, I ended up 12 miles away in the city of Bromley.

By the time I reached my hotel, l was super hang-gry and just wanted to sit down to relax and eat the only available thing in the vending machine: M&M's.

But, I realized that I left my "Hello My Name is Big Dave" sign at the hotel's front desk and had to retrieve it.

When I reached the desk, a British couple "feeling no pain" was checking in. As I grabbed my sign, the guy from the couple slurred out, "What's this sign all about."

I crabbily snapped that I was hugging the world, and, as soon as I did, his face lit up.

"Hugging the world…that's brilliant…tell me more!!"

His happiness may have been booze-fueled, but it came off as genuine and brightened my mood as I fielded questions from him, his girlfriend, and even the front desk clerk.

After hugging everyone, I made a move to go to my room, and the guy asked, "Have you met the Queen yet??"

"Uhh…No," I replied.

"Well, bow down," he said.

Going with the flow, I bowed my head a bit, but this guy was short. He was so short that I needed to get lower, and he belted out, "More!"

With everyone now giggling at our height disparity, he said, "Ehh…a little more."

I again obliged until I was practically genuflecting, and he said, "Ahhh, perfect!!…Well, Big Dave, I Knight Thee!!!"

With that, he kissed the top of my head and followed up with, "I don't know if you'll ever meet the Queen, but I think that's what she'd do if she met you: Now go hug the world, you big mother!!" he said with a hearty laugh.

The Idiot's Lantern

Bromley UK. 2019

While speaking with a rail worker in the Bromley Rail Station outside of London, a man who was eavesdropping on my conversation asked "why" I was hugging people worldwide.

A bit taken aback by this guy interrupting my conversation, I said, "I imagine that when my time is up, I'm going to be asked, 'What did you do for the world around you?' And, I want to be able to say something other than that I told a lot of dirty jokes."

The man then shook his head affirmatively and stepped closer to place his hand atop my forearm and said, "I've been listening, and you are doing a fine job. I TRULY HOPE that I am not the guy who dies ONE SECOND after you and has to come up with a better reply than yours because then; I am proper fucked."

We laughed about his response, and I stated that I would post this on my Instagram page.

"Instagram??...Instagram??...You mean the idiot's lantern?!" he contemptuously said with a full-on British accent—which made it sound super-funny.

Just hearing the word "Instagram" made him unleash a verbal torrent against social media, the Kardashians, posts about people falling, fake stories, and the internet overall.

As he referred to it, the "web of nonsense" is "filled with idiots prattling about their lives!!"

This man probably would still be talking on that platform if I hadn't derailed his rant by extending my hand, smiling and sarcastically stating, "Hi, I'm Dave, and I'm an idiot who hugs the world and then posts about it on the web. Can I get a hug??"

We began laughing again, but he stopped abruptly and flatly said, "Well, I guess that you'd have to be a bit of an idiot to do what you're doing now, wouldn't you??...Well, not a full-on idiot but at least someone with the ideology and resilience of a child and...well, not a child so much but kind of dim to the world.."

He went on to give worse examples with each sentence and would still be talking if I hadn't cut him off by smiling and saying, "Ya know what, let's just hug."

He agreed, we embraced, and afterward, he said, "A hug—that really is a great way to end a chat!"

"Yeah, it is."

Du jour

Paris, France. 2019

Have you ever committed to a task and then have one of those, "wait, I didn't think this through too well," moments before beginning that task? That describes my moments before entering the NewSoul Food restaurant in Paris.

Because it involves spending a lot of time researching locations, and convincing people of my intentions—establishing a "place to embrace" is never easy. But the manager at this popular African and Caribbean eatery made things too easy for me by responding to my email within a day. His note was short and sweet:

> *It will be an honour to welcome the Big Dave in order to*
> *continue your Hug—High5 mission.*

RUDY L.

I was so excited to get his confirmation that I didn't even follow my own protocols by scheduling a follow-up call with him and instead focused on securing "Hug-Hubs" for my itinerary's remaining cities: Dublin, Belfast, London, Rome, Tel Aviv, and Jerusalem.

Language wasn't an issue while hugging people in Ireland, Northern Ireland, or The UK. But, as I struggled to make small talk with a cab driver on the way to the cafe, it dawned on me that language could be a considerable barrier now. I do not know ANY French. I mean, after eating a sandwich on French bread with some French fries and French kissing my date—it's Au revoir!

So, after lamenting why I took Latin over French in high school for a few moments, I took a deep breath and entered the restaurant.

Now there was another problem.

Because we only communicated via email, I had no idea what Rudy, the cafe owner, looked like, so I looked around and took a spot in the to-go line with my Big Dave Hugs the World sign.

With the food smelling great, patrons smiling and laughing, and 90's R&B background music, all of my senses were stimulated, and I fell in love with the place. While enjoying the vibe and trying to figure out the best dish on the menu, a woman approached me with a big smile and said, "Why are you acting like a customer?? Hug People!!"

Ronel was the smiling woman's name, and she was the restaurant's hostess. After hugging me, I said, "you're fluent! Thank god because I don't know much French."

"Don't worry," she said, still smiling, "The owners were scared because of their English."

I may not have known what Rudy looked like, but he knew me. Before Ronel could introduce us, he exclaimed, "Hey!!!!!! It's the Big Brother Hug!! Brother Dave, it is good to see you!! What do you want to do first, hug, or eat??"

"What a great question..why can't everyone greet me like that," I thought.

Nodding my head to Mark Morrison's "Return of the Mack," I elected to begin hugging people, and, as I did the music was turned down, Rudy began making a loud announcement to the restaurant.

Without a clue as to what was going on, I asked Ronel what he was saying.

"Oh, there's a new addition to the menu."

"What is it?" I asked

"You!!...your hugs and high5s now come with every order."

And just like that, the cafe's vibe got even better—and not because of anything I did. The atmosphere was enhanced because some patrons thought their hugs were the menu's new addition and began offering each other embraces.

A few people walked up and hugged Rudy.

And other people began translating a bit of my story and mission for others and approached me with a smile and their arms outstretched.

In the end, I didn't have to worry too much about communication because the language du jour was hugs, high5s, smiles, and 90s tunes.

That night, Paris was the city of Lights and Hugs—and it was beautiful!!

The World Needs Your Smile

Jerusalem, Israel. 2019

What would you ask for if you had God's attention for a moment?

Though I've prayed before, that question never came to mind until I was standing before the Western Wall in Jerusalem.

Being in this one place where so many religions began and seeing so many people from around the planet praying to their belief limits, and faith levels was something I've never experienced.

I felt something deeply spiritual—almost sacred.

That feeling amplified as I stood at the Wall and saw tiny pieces of paper jammed into every crevice within the rocks. Touching the Wall and knowing that each scrap of paper was representative of someone's prayer and someone's dream was compelling to me. Knowing that each piece of paper was the sacred ask of an individual turned my time there into an experience.

I didn't have a prayer to put into the Wall but didn't want my divine moment to slip by—so I thought for a moment and then went through my pockets to grab my business cards.

On one side of my business cards, I have all of my contact information.

On the other side, I have different phrases written on them like Hugs Heal, Thank You For Your Smile, and Big Dave Big Hug. One of my cards even has a "hug coupon" written on the back of it.

I rifled through my cards until I found the one that expressed what I would say to God if I had his attention for a just moment and placed it in the Wall.

"The World Needs Your Smile."

Tikkun Olam

Tel Aviv, Israel. 2019

Years ago, my friend Rachel referred to me as Tikkun Olam—Hebrew for; Repairer of the World.

I don't believe I'm deserving of such lofty praise. But I will say that, since 2001 I have been doing all I can to positively connect with people and make the world a better place and doing so through a simple hug.

While a hug and high5 may be a simple act that is over in a moment, the planning of that embrace can be quite an undertaking.

First, I have to research a city to find it's most populated areas.

Then, I reach out to places in these areas that are open to the public and generally open to good vibes like: elder care facilities, coffee shops, yoga studios, gyms, and such.

Next, I follow up with calls to all of these places to assure people that I am not an asylum escapee. After assuring my sanity and having secured a "Place to Embrace," I work out the logistical details of my mode of travel and lodging accommodations—that can range from being in a hotel to sleeping in a rental car.

After that I try to promote the event through social media and generally make myself available to hug and high5 people for about 5 hours.

In terms of paying for things, I use a combination of my own money and crowdfunding platforms like GoFundMe.

This is just a broad overview of the prep-work needed for me to hug and high5 and I apologize if you were expecting sexier. But like Dorothy when she discovered the Wizard's truth, if you look behind the Hug and High5 curtain, all you'll find is me—an old, foul-mouthed, black man.

Thus, the last night of a tour is always the most memorable because it's when I finally get to relax, reflect, and celebrate everything.

On the last night of my Big Dave Hugs Europe and Israel Tour, I grabbed a snack in a Tel Aviv convenience store. While in line, I struck up a conversation with a couple next to me, and after sharing my story and a hug, I asked them for a picture when they left the store.

They said, 'yes,' and while waiting outside, I recalled all of the planning, time, international calls, emails, logistics, money, and everything else that went into constructing this tour.

During this moment I thought of everything that occurred within the tour— like the many presuppositions people continuously put in my head that had me doubting whether I would be able to embrace anyone.

The cycle of stereotypes was crazy.

The Dublin'ers called the people in Belfast "savages"—who in turn called the Brits "stuck up"—who said that the Parisians weren't going to even speak to me because I didn't know any French—who looked disgusted when I mentioned that I was going to Italy.

It seemed that the ONLY thing that everyone agreed upon was that my "hug act" was going to fail in Israel completely.

"The Israelis don't trust anyone, and they certainly aren't going to trust YOU," one person emphatically exclaimed.

Yet, after hearing all of that and all of the prep work and crossing so many cultural, language, physical, political, and social barriers—I was standing and smiling on a Tel Aviv street—prepared to celebrate a trip that was a success beyond even my loftiest measure.

A rush of achievement practically had me in tears as all of these moments and memories flashed through my head at a dizzying pace. I couldn't wait to hug the couple again as they exited.

Bear hugging both of them; I said, "Thank you. Thank you for your time. Thank you for your smile. Thank you for my moment. Thank you!!"

My emotions took over, and I couldn't stop myself from blurting out some of the stories and beautiful encounters I had on this trip and then thanked them again through very teary eyes.

The woman looked at me and said, "But...I didn't do anything but hug you."

"But, that's what I've predicated the last 18 years of my life on. Your hug means the world to me."

At that point, she and her husband began crying, and we shared one more group embrace. While wiping away a tear, the husband said, "...and to think I didn't want to come to the store with you: I would've missed all of this."

The woman playfully punched her husband in the arm and said, "Seeeeeee, you should listen to me more often!"

I love this picture because I can feel all of the emotion in one glance.

Postscript: I ended up hugging 1006 people in two weeks on my Big Dave Hugs Europe and Israel Tour.

Shana Tova, Allen Iverson

Tel Aviv, Israel. 2019

In a cafe directly outside of my hotel in Tel Aviv, a barista loved my mission as soon as he heard it.

"I love what you're selling, man," he said with a big smile and even refused to serve a customer until they embraced me.

We became fast-friends over coffee, but what "sealed the deal" of our bond was my being from Philadelphia. Upon hearing me say "Philly," he yelled—and I mean YELLED—"Iverson!!!!!! Iverson!!!! I-Ver-Son!!"

Allen Iverson was a six-foot, skinny NBA Hall of Fame guard for the Philadelphia 76ers known for his fearless play and heart. Allen had a crossover dribble that would make even the best defenders look silly. The barista said that he'd practice Allen's cross-over move all the time.

Stepping from behind the counter and balling up a rag as if it were a basketball, he described how special it was to completely cross-over an opponent once in a game.

"My coach was angry because I missed the shot but, fuck that guy—I didn't care, for that moment: I WAS Iverson and it was beautiful!! Shaq was bigger!! Kobe was better. But, no one had Iverson's heart."

The passion within his words "I WAS Iverson" gave me a chill because I could see and feel how important it was for him. I felt honored to have him share such a memory with me, and every time I walked past the cafe, he'd yell something to me:

- "Big Man, do you remember the Lakers/Trailblazer series??"
- "Hug Man, watch this," pointing to some highlights he had cued up on his phone.
- "Big Hug, name your all-time centers?"

I grew to love walking past him because I wanted to see just how many different nicknames he could call me.

The day before I left to return home, I saw him walking away from the cafe with a small suitcase and eating a sandwich.

"Hug, where are you going?" he asked.

"To my hotel?...Where are you going?" I replied.

He said that he was going to his parents for a few days for Rosh Hashanah and invited me to come with him. "You of all people shouldn't be alone—you should be surrounded by love and breaking bread with family."

As much as I appreciated the offer, I couldn't accept it because I was leaving early the next morning.

"Take care of yourself," I said with a hug and began to step away.

"N-n-n-n-no!" he declared as he grabbed my arm and looked at me as if he had a brilliant idea. "I know what we'll do."

With that, he took his sandwich entirely out of its wrapper and ripped it in half and handed it to me.

Nodding as if to say "eat," I took a bite, and he said, "SEE...We broke bread... there is always a way!"

We hugged again, and afterward, I placed my hand atop my heart and said, "Yeah, there's always a way, brother. Keep practicing that cross-over. Shana Tova."

"Shana Tova" is Hebrew for "a good year" and said during Rosh Hashanah—it is also a phrase that the barista was practicing with me the day before.

"Heyyyy!!! You remembered!!!! Shana Tova, Big Man."

I Got Another Lyft

Philadelphia, PA. 2020

While running an errand one Saturday afternoon, I passed a hot dog stand, and a man standing in line smiled at me and said, "Hey, Big Man! Do you remember me?...I was your Lyft driver a few months ago."

He seemed vaguely familiar, so I just nodded my head and said "OK" while the guy kept talking.

"...I was having a bad day that day, and you just listened to me vent, and then you ended up talking to me. And, you know what??...By the end of the ride, I felt so much better about things that when you got out of the car and said 'let's hug this out'; I did... I felt special until I looked you up online and saw that this is what you do for people all over the world and then I felt REALLY special. Keep doing what you're doing; it's beautiful."

With that, he ran to his double-parked car.

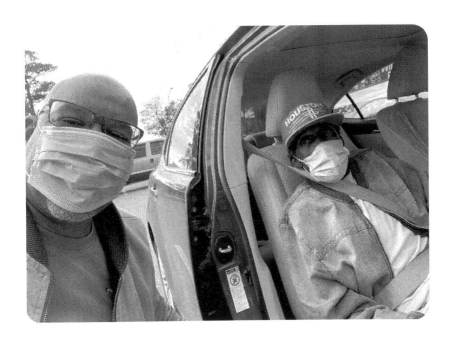

BBQ & Blessings

Houston, Texas. 2020

I wasn't family upon entering Gatlin's BBQ but certainly felt that way leaving.

I planned to meet Ben, a friend and ex-Marine I met on one of my previous hug tours, for lunch, but one question changed it all.

I asked the older woman serving us if Gatlin's was a part of a chain.

"No, baby, this is it."

That question was all it took for this proud mother, named Theresa, to speak of working at her son Gregory's restaurant. She also shared that Gregory approached her with the notion of opening a BBQ restaurant 11 years ago while he was still attending Rice University, promising that it, would just be "part-time."

"I'm still waiting for the 'part-time' part to kick in," she said with a chuckle.

After sharing her backstory, she remarked that she noticed the New Jersey tags on my car and asked what I was doing in Houston.

As I revealed my story and mission of my 48 state #SmileWithBigDave Tour, I could tell that Theresa's—"Mother Theresa" as she's affectionately known— smile beamed.

With eyes that squinted a bit as her cheeks rose and masked mouth grinned, I felt her happiness and heard her glee as she said, "God is good and is acting through you. I'm gonna introduce you to my son. Now eat!!"

As Ben and I sat to eat and catch up, a woman ordering food from Theresa waved at me and yelled, "I hear you're doing good things!!!"

"I guess; C'mon down and sit!" I yelled back.

The woman, named Carolyn, obliged and, after chatting, said she'd like me to meet her brother who was suffering from cancer, and she just picked up from chemotherapy.

"He can't eat it, but he wants bbq, and I would love for him to meet you and get some of your energy!"

I agreed and began walking out, and as we left, Mother Theresa shouted, "Y-y-you aren't leaving, are you??"

"No, Ma'am, we're coming right back!" Ben and I shouted.

Outside, I walked to Carolyn's car and met her brother.

Gaunt from chemo and too weak to even really sit up straight, I fist-bumped his hand and asked if I could pray with him.

"I'll take all the prayers I can get," he said.

Dropping to a knee, I took his hand and said that we would both say a prayer in silence because I don't pray often and didn't know what prayer was best.

Before bowing my head, I said, "Besides, two prayers are better than one, right?"

"MMM-MM," he said, nodding his head affirmatively and giving me a weak smile.

Standing up, I saw Carolyn standing in front of the car holding Ben's hand and heard her excitedly say, "I knew you were a good man. I could FEEL it!! Thank you."

As Ben and I reentered Gatlin's, it was like walking into a friend's home. Mother Theresa introduced me to the whole Gatlin family and staff, customers at other tables, and even took their framed 'first dollar' off the wall to show me.

The energy now within Gatlin's was amazingly harmonious and only got warmer when I told Theresa that she and my mother shared the same name.

With a spark in her eye, she said, "That makes sense. God is taking care of you by sending a bunch of mothers to look after you. God's got you, baby!!"

But it was soon time for me to leave, and after giving me a to-go container of BBQ, Theresa took my hand and proclaimed, "You are family. Now go out and do your work and make the world smile!!"

Once outside, Ben just looked at me and said, "T-t-t-that was beautiful," and gave me a huge hug.

Looks Like We Made It!

Philadelphia, PA. May 2021

The picture and moment accompanying this chapter was a long time in the making.

You see, for years, I've been seeing this elderly man and his home health aid taking their daily walks and waving to them each time.

No matter the weather conditions or time of day—this man would pause his walk to give me a smile and a wave.

Because of COVID, I never saw this after the lockdown began in March 2020 and feared that I possibly lost my "wave" partner forever.

But on one sunny afternoon in May 2021, I saw this man and his aide walking by and immediately yelled, "My Man!!" as loud as I could. Then, whipping around as fast as a 90-year-old man can, he locked eyes with me and smiled. No mask could've hidden that grin.

It was a good moment that only grew into something more because the man steadied himself to give me two thumbs-up, and I returned his gesture.

Our moment continued blossoming when the man then blew me a kiss, and again I did the same.

Then, like an excited child, he pulled his mask away from his face so I could see his full smile and gave me an air-hug.

I returned his air-hug, but this man was not finished with our moment.

He began shuffling over to me and yelling, "I thought I lost you!"

"Nah, man, we both made it," I yelled back with a huge grin.

Now standing before each other, I raised my hand to celebrate our moment with a High5. But, this man had his own ideas and reached his hand up to meet mine and interlock our fingers.

Now laughing, he happily repeating my words, "We both made it. We both made it."

After a year of being separated from hugs, and human contact, this was so much more than just a high5.

This was a beautiful moment.

It's Your Turn

You are everyone's
HERO — even if they
don't know it yet! Keep
spreading the Love
this world needs!
— Mark♡

All Over the World!

September 12 will now be officially recognized as National Hug and High5 Day.

I received this great honor because of my embracing efforts, and looking back to September 12, 2001, I can honestly say I never saw any of this coming—none of it.

20 years ago, all I believed was that I was a man with a dead friend.

But through an embrace's pursuit, I discovered I was so much more; a cross-continental cyclist, a motivator, a writer, a storyteller, a filmmaker, a life coach, and more.

As I said in this book's opening chapter, acquiring a simple hug has been my portal for becoming a better man.

So with this 99th and final chapter, I would like to speak about something even more vital to the world than my hugs: YOUR TREASURE.

Right now, the world's burgeoning unrest and incivility has stoked people's fears and anxiety to a high point.

And with these last few paragraphs, I hope to convince you to join me in opening your own 'treasure chest' and sharing its contents with others to make the world a happier place.

Let me stop you before you say that you aren't a hugger—you don't have to be—that's my thing.

As I said, this isn't about me; this about you sharing your talent and ability. There are thousands of ways you can contribute, but here are a few simple examples to consider:

> You can always give a dollar to a cause you believe in, or even better, you can volunteer your time with that charity.

> You can take a meal to a senior citizen or even better, invite them to eat with your family once a month.

> You can offer someone a ride to work or, even better, a ride home.

> You can become a big brother or a mentor; it really is an experience that will change both of your lives.

You can edit a chapter of someone's book—Lord knows, I needed that.

You can offer a tutorial on something—Lord knows, I needed that too.

You can help someone fundraise for an event.

You can mentor a younger coworker or help edit someone's resumé—everyone needs help with that.

You are strong in places where others aren't, and I ask you to give what you got!

Take it from me—throughout the last 20 years, many of my friends have stepped up to lend a hand, tutor me, give me a bike, rent me a car, edit an article, and a myriad of other things so I could continue on to hug, high5 and help others smile.

Sharing their treasure kept me going.

So please do what you can to help others because the world needs your gifts and your smile more than ever and after sharing that treasure, write to me and tell me about it:

Thehumanhigh5@Gmail.com

Instagram @thehumanhigh5

+1 267.252.1974

Or even better, find me in Philly—it's on every map—and let's sit down, socially distanced, if that's still a thing so that you can tell me all about it.

Thank you so much for reading this book—it means more than you know.

Hugs—High5s—Love—Respect

BIG DAVE

Afterword

So…What do you think?

The story of Big Dave at this point probably seems like a lot of things: heartwarming, annoying, funny, sad, healing, crazy, and/or exaggerated.
It's not.

I haven't been there for any of these stories, but *someone* has. There are people all around this world who have met David and lived these stories. Beyond that, there are even more who have heard him tell these stories. Because—trust me—if you ever have (or will) meet Big Dave, he will tell you a story or two.

He clearly has enough of them.

When David was getting ready to publish this book electronically I walked into the room where he was (almost quietly) working to see him how I have so often seen him: a large presence curled over a small laptop, glasses off, intent on his key strokes and the screen. After almost ten years of working with Dave I could tell something was off right away.

"What's goin' on?" I said, leaning against a doorway to the conference room where he was working.

"Dude. I just lost everything."

"Wait, what?"

"Yeah man, this program…I saved it last night…I opened this document at work…tried to open it again…and it says the file can't be found."

Well shit.

Those close to Dave know that his ideas and plans for hugging the world are a lot like an iceberg: by the time we find out about them they are nearly unavoidable and go way deeper than we could imagine. But with that comes

323

"Dave-in-Action." Hard work, high-speed thinking, delusions of grandeur, planning for failure, laughs, worries.

At the point that Dave lost his work formatting this book the first time, I didn't see much concern. Dave can handle a lot of different shit getting thrown at him…But it happened again.

And again.

"Dude, this program sucks," he would tell me. "I just spent all day again trying to fix this."

When it came time to make the print version Dave and I took a lot of time to try and get it right. We wanted an experience for the reader that could show highs and lows, love in the face of love, and love in the face of hate. I offered to work on the book with him at the least to save him from losing his work anymore.

This story may start with *Travelling at the Speed of Life* or earlier. It may start on September 11th, 2001; but for me it doesn't really need a start, as long as it doesn't have an ending.

Big Dave can be a lot of things—and you have seen him be a lot of things in this book—but more than anything he is your biggest supporter.

You.

YOU.

Yesterday I stood with David at the 9/11 Memorial at the World Trade Center. Dave—where he is probably most uncomfortable—stood at Kevin Bowser's name where a young man was standing to his left. I backed away to give them both their moment; clearly, they were both at that exact spot because someone close to them was memorialized on that plaque. Leaning against the tree a few feet behind them I watched Dave start to speak to this stranger as they both gestured and pointed to the names on the plaque. I couldn't make out what they were saying—and frankly, I didn't want to—then I heard Dave say, "Do you want a hug?"

That's who Dave is.

There were plenty of cameras and crews, and people who wanted to share their presence at the memorial that day, but Dave was there with nothing. Just reaching out to whoever needed it.

Another man joined us and as soon as Dave saw him his shoulders relaxed, he smiled and said, "Dude" and quickly embraced his new visitor. "Thank you for coming," was all I heard him say when they hugged; then the man backed away as I had done and stood next to me.

He and I chatted for a while when he told me that he met David when they worked at a Center City Philadelphia sporting goods store. He was just a high school student, Dave, a few years his senior.

On the train home that day from New York I thought about how here he was: a man who decided to reach out to the world with nearly nothing but the hope to make *your* day better because he lost a friend 20 years ago at that exact spot. His mentor was gone, but he stood with the three of us trying to better our lives from a position of the "elder in the room." The same way I imagine the twins were to him. The way Kevin may have wanted *him* to be.

Measured. Thoughtful. Funny. And embracing.

David's mission started 20 years ago today. While the world may not be a kinder place, I hope hearing Big Dave's stories has at least shown you that the world *can be* a kinder place.

And that it doesn't take much.

Joseph Stingle
9.11.21

Shout Outs

This book contains stories that span my life, so there are many people to thank. Here are just a few.

Aimee Glocke: Thank you for introducing your students to my world.

Andrea Zak: Thank you for never forgetting my birthday.

Anne Burke: Thank you for not letting me tap out.

Andrew and Ariel: Thank you for believing in my story.

Avelina Espilita: There's a special place in heaven for you.

Barry Burst: Thank you for introducing me to some great Real Estate.

Brandon, Thaon, and Laila: Be ever confident and always remember that you can do anything and everything.

Brian Howard: Thanks for the cover!

Brian Rodgers: Because of you. Austin is home for me too.

Brian Zieger: I hope I never need you, but I am glad I got you.

Carline Raphael: Thank you for showing me the nobility within enduring.

Carnell "Cave-Man" Baugh: You're a motherfucker too.

Catriona Kennedy: Thanks for seeing past my volume.

Cedric Ulad: Coworker to friend to boss to brother, thank you.

Charlie "mother fuckin" Davidson: There is only one President.

Cherie McKay: Thank you for helping introduce me to the world.

Chris Gabello: Thank you for helping me see life's bigger picture.

327

Cyndi Kwan: Thanks for reading my first draft.

David Devan: Your substance, strength, and style always inspire.

Dawud Anyabwile: When Bother Man sleeps at night, he dreams of being you.

Denise Sistrunk: God only knows how many times angels have kissed you.

Dr. Christa Heyward: Thanks for putting clothes on.

Dr. Matthew S Johnson: Fuck cancer.

Dr. Merida Grant: Thanks for showing me how to focus.

Duke Cannon and Christina Connelly: Thank you for taking my call and passing on my message—you changed the whole game!!

Eric Crawford: I can't wait to collaborate on the trailer for my movie.

Frank Schinchimini: Thank you for believing in me when other bike shops wouldn't.

George Stock: One can learn a lot about life by saying "good morning' to people in a coffee shop.

Greg Perry: Nothing in the gym has been as much fun since you left. You really did cover the ground you stood on.

Ingrid Vanderveldt: Thank you for letting me talk.

James Turner: Always calm—Always competent—Always there.

Jarrod Lewis: You saw it all in the beginning.

Jeff Kyem: You are one of the world's greatest Haters and I love it!! You make the world laugh. You make the world better.

Jen Fox: I can't wait 'til the next Friends-giving!!

Jim Caple: You really did alter my trajectory.

Joe Stingle: You may be Don Draper. I may be Roger Sterling. Thank God we aren't Pete or Peggy ☺

Johanna Blyth: You were the first person to buy *Traveling at the Speed of Life*—time for another purchase!

Johnny Cash: Thanks for showing me that the most challenging decisions are sometimes the best decisions.

Kallan Resnick: Twenty years later, your strength and determination remain unrivaled and motivating.

Kedrick Johnson: Thank you for your brotherhood.

Kellen Carter: You are one of a kind but stink at returning calls :)

Kelvin Bowser: Thank you for being the first cool guy I ever met.

Korinna Shaw: Thanks for reading my profile.

Larry Leonard: Thank you for towing me.

Larry McMichael: You have another brother in me.

Leigh, Elizabeth, Amelia, Benny, and Chico: 5106 always makes me happier.

Leo Holt: You gave me the best marching orders ever, "...just go out and do good, Dave."

Lynne Hernandez: Thanks for reminding me to get to the point.

Malini Sekhar: You are my Craigslist Angel.

Mark Wallace: Thank you for showing me that it's never too late to become who you want.

Judge Mary Porter: Thank you for always riding with me.

Mary Sandor: Thank you for helping me deliver my message.

Matthew Siembeda: Your support got this whole ball rolling.

Maurice Baynard: Shit, STILL, don't stop!!

Melina Bell: Thanks for showing me what discipline can achieve.

Michelle Price: Your office is my office—it doesn't happen without you.

Miia Melkoniemi: Thanks for accepting my apology.

Mike Ambrose: I look forward to our 1.8 hugs per year.

Miriam George: I wished upon a star, and there you were.

Nancy, Dennis, Sake, Simon, and Ziva: Everyone needs a second mom like you, Nancy.

Natalie Martin: Thanks for always sounding excited to hear my voice.

Natalie Panaia: Thanks for opening your heart and stores to me.

Pete Madden: You don't just do things; you do things right.

Poppy Renee: Continue your parent's work of making the world a better place—and always remember there's love in their every embrace.

Priscilla Coblentz: Red is everyone's favorite color.

Rachel Gans: I think that you are a hero too.

Ramith Nukrumah: You were always original—never off-brand.

Reese Blair: The world is a brighter place when you share your insight.

Rich Phillips: The WORLD'S FIRST ever Hug & High5 Festival doesn't happen without you!

Ryder & Jaxson: Always appeal to your better angels and hug your parents often because they're fantastic people.

Sara Trohaugh: My human ray of sunshine.

Scott Brookens and Steve Ebersole: Long live the Room of Doom!

Scott Miller: Uighur, please.

Shelley Meaney: Thanks for your trust.

Sherri Franklin: Your words and wisdom still keep me evolving.

Sheryl Leonard: You are in my head every time I write.

Sophia Counelis: Se Agapó!

Stan Wilkes: Thanks for the offer, but I am good.

Stephanie Falkenstein: I look forward to the next book club meeting.

Sue Prant: New Year's Eve in Topeka was fun.

Suzy Q: Thanks for the birthday cake.

The Birenbaum's: Thank you for making me a part of your family.

Thomas Puleo: Music, photography, coffee; is there anything you can't do?

Thor Curran: Thank you for asking me to stay for dinner and always hug your parents.

Tracy Sylvester: No one is as smart or funny—thank you for making me better.

Wendy Laurijssens: Thanks for the pictures; they still make me smile.

Zoe Bisk: Your smile has shined my way from Germany to Washington, New York, and all the way around the world to Australia.

Advantage Rental Car: You stepped up when others didn't, and because of that, tens of thousands of people from around the world got hugs, high5s, and good vibes!

Hilton Hotels: You've had a place for me to stay no matter where I hugged.

Keen Sandals: As one woman said when she looked at my Keen sandals, "He should be out actin' like Jesus; he's already wearin' his shoes!!"

Specialized Bicycles and Philipp Moeller:
Thank you for the bike and for believing in my potential.

For those companies and entities who passed on my story: it's not too late to get on board, but it's gonna run you a couple of dollars!

Waldron Academy, Central High School, and Temple University: Thank you for molding my mind.

Jeff McFadden, Pat Tobin and The Union League of Philadelphia Membership/Staff: Thanks for reinforcing the tenet that our ideas and the drive to pursue them are the most remarkable parts of who we are.

Made in the USA
Middletown, DE
15 October 2023

40632941R00205